Moms encouraging moms to know the love of Christ

Dearest Friend,

We are so glad you have joined us on this journey as we learn what it means to abide in Jesus! *The Wise Woman Abides* devotional workbook will encourage you as you grow in receiving, trusting, and savoring the living water offered by your Savior. Sister, Jesus is calling you to walk closely with Him this season as He prepares a harvest of His fruits in your heart (John 15:4)!

Be prepared for the Holy Spirit to speak to your heart as you walk closely with Jesus, study His Word, delight in His ways, and trust in the goodness of His character. Jesus wants to cultivate new things in your relationship with Him, your marriage, and your role as a mother! His love for you is infinitely deep and His plans for you are full of hope. Rest in Him, dear one, and abide in His love and peace.

There are three essential components to this study, designed to encourage you in your roles as a Christian woman, wife, and mother: Prayer, Bible Study, and Mom Tips.

Prayer: We believe prayer changes everything, and we encourage you to prayerfully consider finding someone who you can pray with once a week over the phone, preferably someone who is doing this Bible study as well. This one habit of praying with a prayer partner will change your life!

Bible Study: Included in your workbook each week are three Bible studies (you choose which days to complete them). They begin with Scriptures to read and meditate on as well as an invitation to pray and fellowship with your beautiful Savior. The studies always end with "Questions to Ponder" and a "Faith-Filled Idea." These are meant to stir your heart and mind into action, and bring lasting, godly change into your everyday life! We pray the Holy Spirit draws you into a deeper relationship with your Heavenly Father as you actively endeavor to know Him more.

Mom Tips: We are so excited to share our "Mom Tips" with you each week! These practical ideas are meant to enhance your life and role as a Christian wife, mom, discipler of your children, homemaker, and friend. You can pray about which tips to try and check them off as you accomplish them. Completing them all or doing only one is just fine!

This workbook is designed to help you become the wise woman who abides in Christ. Jesus desires for you to lean into Him and His love each day. He will fill you with His perfect peace as your mind is focused on Him and you are trusting in His ways (Isaiah 26:3). As you walk through this study, you will engage yourself in God's Word and open your heart to Him in prayer. Your life will forever be changed by making a habit of abiding in your Savior!

We pray for you to encounter Jesus, to grow in spiritual wisdom and understanding as you actively participate in our study—*The Wise Woman Abides.*

Blessings and love,

The Help Club for Moms Team

The Wise Woman Abides

What does it mean to Abide?

As we ponder what it means to abide, we realize this concept can be unfamiliar and hard to understand. Abiding in Christ means to stay connected to Jesus and trust Him in all things.

Understanding God's sovereignty in our lives produces a beautiful response in our hearts. Knowing we can trust the God of the Universe who goes before us, makes a way for us, and knows the future, causes us to take a step back and rest. It frees us to follow Him and stay the course with a blindfold on, knowing that wherever He takes us is going to be good and well worth the trek.

Trusting Jesus with the circumstances in our lives is no easy task. Learning to abide in Christ is a lifelong journey. With the help of the Holy Spirit, we can learn to abide by drawing near to Jesus and staying in His presence.

God has given each of us a different family puzzle and so many areas where we can practice abiding in Him. When our daughter is struggling with anger issues, abiding is embracing her while trusting God, and not constantly complaining about why we have such a hard time with her. When we are arguing with our spouse and it seems never-ending, abiding is loving him through the pain and not wishing for a better husband. When we envy our neighbor's possessions, abiding is knowing God is good and He will provide what we need.

Friends, as you ask the Lord to help you to "abide in Him," be prepared to gaze through a new lens at your circumstances! God has a way of shedding light and love on whatever He touches. As you stick close to Jesus and bear your circumstances with patience, grace, and hope, Jesus will be at work in your life!

We pray these pages are a blessing to you and the call to be a "Wise Woman who Abides" would be life-changing to you and to those in your home.

"Abide in me, and I in you. As the branch cannot bear fruit by itself, unless it abides in the vine, neither can you, unless you abide in me" (John 15:4 ESV).

With Love,
Krystle and the Help Club for Moms Team

Table of Contents

The Wise Woman Abides

Table of Contents

All Mom Tips authored by the Help Club for Moms' "Mom Tips" Team

Love of God

~ Week One ~

Hello, Help Club Mamas!

I'm so excited to begin our new Book, *The Wise Woman Abides,* with you and dive into our first topic: The Love of God!

The love of God! Does it get any more beautiful, wonderful, and never-ending than that? Can we even grasp its greatness? God's great love is illustrated many times for us in the Bible—our source of Truth. One of the most quoted verses is, "For God so loved the world that he gave his one and only Son, that whoever believes in him shall not perish but have eternal life" (John 3:16). Also, in Romans 5:8 (NLT), "But God showed his great love for us by sending Christ to die for us while we were still sinners." Additionally, in 1 John 4:16 (ESV), "So we have come to know and to believe the love that God has for us. God is love, and whoever abides in love abides in God, and God abides in him."

Now is the time for each of us to ponder the concept of abiding in God's great love for us! Take a moment to reflect on "how wide and long and high and deep is the love of Christ" (Ephesians 3:18).

One way to help us see God's love for us is to change our perspective on how we view Him. Is He a far-off, abstract "being" that just oversees our life, or is He closer, nearer to us, with us—as our Father, our Daddy?

Ironically, it was during a conversation I had with my own dad that I began to grasp this concept of God as my *Father,* my *Daddy.* We discussed how there are times when we call out to God and may use different names for Him: Jesus, Lord, Father, Abba, etc. Then, it dawned on me, we cry out to Him at times just as a child does for its parents: Mom, Mama, Mommmmyyyy. As mothers, we know that each of those names, and the way they are said, mean something different. We can tell when our children are sad, hurt, happy, or fearful.

Isn't it time we converse with God this way? Call out to Him: "Daddddyyy I need you..." or "Dad, I think I may have just messed up." God becomes closer to us this way. We begin to view Him as someone who understands us, and someone who we can depend on when we need comforting, advice, and yes, love. In Jesus' own words in Matthew 6:8b (NLT), "...for your Father knows exactly what you need even before you ask him!"

No matter what our relationship is like with our earthly father, our heavenly Father wants to have our *love* and *know* us! After all, we are called in John 15:9 (ESV) to abide in His love, and the way we do that is to explore the depths of our Father's great love for us.

Blessings and love,
Kristall Willis and the Help Club for Moms Team

> ❝ *There is no friendship, no love, like that of the parent for the child.* ❞
> ~ Henry Ward Beecher

Mom Tips

"I am the vine; you are the branches. If you remain in me and I in you, you will bear much fruit..." ~ John 15:5

The Wise Woman Builds Her Spirit

- Get a pad of spiral-bound index cards to keep at your kitchen sink and download a voice recording app on your phone. These tools will be used frequently to help you memorize Scripture.

- Buy a new journal or notebook from the store. Dedicate it as a place to jot down what you are thankful for as you go throughout your days. Even if you only add one or two items a day, you will fill the pages over time! Every so often, come back to it and be reminded of how God is working in your life! Allow your family to get in on it too!

The Wise Woman Loves Her Husband

- Ask your husband how you can pray for him this week. Is he experiencing challenges at work? Can you commit to praying for these challenges to help ease his burden? Remember to listen with an open heart when he shares his concerns with you.

- As a couple, go online to find a love language test to learn how each of you receives love differently. Ask your husband how you can exhibit love toward him and put these ideas into action. Most importantly, be willing to learn when you don't understand his perspective.

The Wise Woman Loves Her Children

- When you say goodnight to your children this week tell them something that they did well. Help them see the gifts God has given them that they use naturally during their day. This encourages your children to know that God is moving in their lives today, not just once they "grow up." Read 1 Timothy 4:12 to show them that they can be an example even to you!

- Consider adding a devotion time with your kids (any age!) this week. Gather a Bible or children's devotional book and some paper (to illustrate what is being read). Have fun together by reading God's Word, acting it out, praying together and for each other, learning a short Bible verse by making up silly actions to go along with it, singing, and talking about the questions your kids have or what God is doing in their lives. Do as much or as little as you want; every bit counts! Have fun! This is a new habit worth forming with your children!

The Wise Woman Cares For Her Home

- Make your bed first thing this week, as soon as you wake up. An easy way to get started is to make one side at a time. Simple, intentional tasks always start the day on a positive note.

- Do the "15-minute pick up" with your children right before your husband comes home. Set a timer for 15 minutes; pick up everything that is out of place and put it away. Focus on the shared living areas of your home and have everyone help. Bless your husband with a picked up house.

> ❝ What do you think? If a man owns a hundred sheep, and one of them wanders away, will he not leave the ninety-nine on the hills and go to look for the one that wandered off? And if he finds it, truly I tell you, he is happier about that one sheep than about the ninety-nine that did not wander off. ❞
>
> ~ Matthew 18:12-13

"And oh, the overwhelming, never-ending, reckless love of God
Oh, it chases me down, fights 'til I'm found, leaves the ninety-nine
And I couldn't earn it, and I don't deserve it, still, You give Yourself away
Oh, the overwhelming, never-ending, reckless love of God..."
~ Cory Asbury

- A big component of the Help Club for Moms is praying with a prayer partner for 10 minutes once a week. If you don't have a prayer partner, pray and ask God to bring her to you!! He is faithful and will provide!

- It's time to meet with your Jesus! Oh, how He loves you and me! Pray today for God to speak to your heart, and help you to feel His love—the wide and long and high and deep love of Jesus (Ephesians 3:18).

- Read today's Scripture out loud slowly. Try to imagine the story in your mind. Ask God to help you see yourself the way He sees you, holy and dearly loved. You are His daughter, a child of the King of Kings. Write down what God speaks to you.

The Reckless Love of God

By: Deb Weakly

Many years ago, during a particularly difficult season in my life, I remember sitting in my then counselor's office and telling her through tears how hard my last week had been and about a few things I had said and done. I will never forget what she said in response to my words, "Wow! You can be impulsive!"

At first, I couldn't believe that what she was saying could possibly be true, but then I started to ponder my conversations and how I had responded. After thinking about it, I realized she was right. I can be reactive and insecure in my thoughts and conversations, especially when I find myself in that deep, dark place of despair and depression.

Can you relate, sister? Are you sometimes impulsive? Do you often respond to people in your life in ways you wish you wouldn't? Well, me too. The struggle is real.

At that point in my life, I remember desperately wanting to run away. Life was just too, too much. Disappointments multiplied, and the next thing I knew, I was driving down the freeway wishing I could get away from it all. One particularly dark day, I distinctly remember crying out to God for help. No, actually, I was screaming out to God for help. All I could say was "Jesus! Jesus! Jesus! Rescue me, Jesus!"

Do you ever feel like you need to be rescued? Do you need God to wrap His holy, loving arms around you and hold you until you can finally stop crying? I do too. He will, dear one. Jesus will rescue you; He will never walk away from you, no matter who gives up on you or what you have said or done. In fact, Jesus goes out of His way to tell you in today's parable (Matthew 18) that "he rejoices more over that one sheep than over the ninety-nine that did not go astray..." Have you ever thought about that? Jesus delights in you, dear lost sheep, more than He does any of the other "sheep" who may have it all together and who have never run away.

Sweet one, you might feel like you have made a hot mess out of your life, but please know that Jesus knows how to make it beautiful. He takes the ashes of your broken life, tills the soil of your heart, and plants a garden of the most fragrant blooms you have ever seen in your life.

That's what Jesus does best: He takes what is broken and fixes it for us. Then, He delights in His precious daughter even more. We give Him our pain; He gives us Himself. Like a child who has recently finished a tantrum, we can exhale deeply in peace, knowing that no matter what is going on around us, the love of Jesus is steadfast and secure.

"Oh, the overwhelming, never-ending, reckless love of God..." He will never give up on you. Come to Him today with your hands open. Give Him your troubles and anxiety, and rest in His care. Trust Him. Let go of everything that you are holding onto—all the things you think will make you happy. Believe me, He will take those dashed dreams of yours and give them back to you so much better than they ever were before. Give Jesus control of your life and your expectations. He is closer than your very breath. Let Him hold you. He will never let you go...ever.

Questions to Ponder

- If you were completely honest, do you feel far away from God? Does it feel like He is nowhere to be found and you are all alone?

- Take a moment to pour out your heart to God. In your journal, write out a personal prayer just like David did in Psalm 13 when he felt far away from God. Write this beautiful portion of Scripture as well. Notice at the end what David says about God.

> *How long, Lord? Will you forget me forever?*
> *How long will you hide your face from me?*
> *How long must I wrestle with my thoughts*
> *and day after day have sorrow in my heart?*
> *How long will my enemy triumph over me?*
>
> *Look on me and answer, Lord my God.*
> *Give light to my eyes, or I will sleep in death,*
> *and my enemy will say, "I have overcome him,"*
> *and my foes will rejoice when I fall.*
>
> *But I trust in your unfailing love;*
> *my heart rejoices in your salvation.*
> *I will sing the Lord's praise,*
> *for he has been good to me.* (Psalm 13)

Did you see that? David finishes lamenting feeling forgotten by God with a true statement: "But I trust in your unfailing love; my heart rejoices in your salvation. I will sing the Lord's praise, for he has been good to me."

If there is one thing I have learned from struggling through dark and depressing times in my life, it's that we need to ponder truth as much as possible. Satan wants us to believe the lies he is speaking into our thoughts. But meditating on the never-changing, always encouraging Word of God will change your heart and mind faster and more permanently than anything else.

Faith-Filled Ideas

One of the best ways to get out of the "pits" of this life is to commit encouraging Scriptures to memory. I would love to share two of my favorites with you. Record these verses on a voice recording app on your phone and write them in dry erase marker on your bathroom mirror until you know them, inside and out. Pray these powerful Scriptures over yourself and your family each day.

And I pray that you, being rooted and established in love, may have power, together with all the Lord's holy people, to grasp how wide and long and high and deep is the love of Christ, and to know this love that surpasses knowledge—that you may be filled to the measure of all the fullness of God. (Ephesians 3:17-19)

I keep asking that the God of our Lord Jesus Christ, the glorious Father, may give you the Spirit of wisdom and revelation, so that you may know him better. I pray that the eyes of your heart may be enlightened in order that you may know the hope to which he has called you, the riches of his glorious inheritance in his holy people, and his incomparably great power for us who believe. That power is the same as the mighty strength he exerted when he raised Christ from the dead... (Ephesians 1:17-20a)

I love these verses because they tell us that we need to pray to understand the love of God. We can't even begin to understand the width, length, depth, and height of it without prayer. Without it, we also cannot understand the power of the Holy Spirit that lives inside of each of us as Christ-followers. After all, it is the same power that raised Jesus Christ from the dead, and it lives inside of you and me!

Oh, and by the way, here's a link to a beautiful song about the reckless love of God: https://www.youtube.com/watch?v=Sc6SSHuZvQE

journal

_____
_____
_____
_____
_____
_____
_____
_____
_____
_____
_____
_____
_____
_____

> " And I pray that you, being rooted and established in love,
> may have power, together with all the Lord's holy people,
> to grasp how wide and long and high and deep is the love of Christ. "
> ~ Ephesians 3:17-18

"God loves each of us as if there were only one of us."
~ St. Augustine

- Good morning my friend! We all want to be moms who point our little ones to Jesus, don't we? Let's get some practical ideas on how to do this today!

- Read Ephesians 3:14-19 and let this passage sink deep into your heart. God loves you, He truly does!

Teaching Your Children About the Love of God

By: Tara Davis

Do you have a hard time comprehending God's love for you? At times, our children struggle with this concept as well. Though children have a special faith that we are called to emulate, they also live with a multitude of easy information at their fingertips. Far off places, mysteries of nature, monumental events in history, all of these are just a library trip or mouse click away. Not much is left unseen, and few mysteries are left unsolved. Knowledge about any subject can be easily obtained and experienced, and the concept of faith in something they cannot see is often foreign. Because of this, experiencing God may not be easy for our children. They can neither see nor touch Him. They will most likely never audibly hear his voice and cannot physically climb up on His lap for a hug after a hard day.

We need to be intentional in *teaching* our children about God's love and in helping His love become tangible to them (Deuteronomy 6:4-9). The truth is it takes a lifetime to learn about God's love. It is something we are all still growing in, but wouldn't you love your children to be leaps and bounds ahead of you in this area? Me too, sister. We must encourage them to develop habits that will enable them to grow in their understanding and acceptance of God's love as they mature.

While I was praying about how to be more intentional with my kids in teaching them the love of Christ, God directed me to simply look in His Word. The Bible has answers to all the questions of our heart (2 Timothy 3:16-17)! So, check out Ephesians 3:14-19 again. Let's pick apart the first few verses for ideas on how to really instill the love of Christ in our children!

- **"Kneel before the Father"** (vs 14) – Have consistent times every day to stop and pray with your children. It is so easy to just rattle off a prayer and go about your day, but try to focus on truly talking to God from your heart. Show your children what it looks like to have a real conversation with their loving Father. They need to learn how to pray from *us*!

- **"The Father, from whom every family derives its name"** (vs 15) – The Bible tells us that God is our Abba Father—our Daddy. Talk to your children about how God is the most loving, perfect Daddy they could imagine!

- **"Strengthen them with power through His Spirit"** (vs 16) – Teach them about the Holy Spirit! Oh, how I want to teach my children about God's amazing power that lives in them! A good start is to simply read a Bible passage about the Holy Spirit and ask your children what they think it means and how it applies to their walks with God. Show your excitement about the Holy Spirit and pray that the Spirit will move in a mighty way in your family and in the hearts of your children. Here are a few passages on the Holy Spirit, but search online to find more: Acts 2:1-5, John 14:16-18, and Romans 8:5-6.

- **"Christ dwells in your heart through faith"** (vs 17) – The primary tool that will bind our children's hearts to the love of God is faith. Romans 10:17 tells us that, "faith comes by hearing, and hearing by the word of God." It is so important that we teach our children how to form the habit of studying and applying God's Word in their lives! This can begin by us reading God's Word to them. As they get older, teach them tools to study God's Word themselves!

- **"You, being rooted and established in love"** (vs 18) – Our children will become rooted in love when they experience our Christ-like love for them! Mamas, we need to work on our kindness (Hosea 11:4) and on being "quick to listen, slow to speak, and slow to become angry" (James 1:19).

Sisters, I encourage you to try a couple ideas this week and to pray that God will direct you in leading your little ones into His loving arms!

Questions to Ponder

· Ask your children about their views on God's love. What did they say? Let these questions stir deeper conversation. Do not be dismayed by doubts that children, especially older children, express. We are their safe places and becoming a disciple of Jesus is sure to come with doubts and questions along the way. Keep pouring into your children and speaking Jesus' truth to their hearts!

Faith-Filled Ideas

I love how Ephesians 3 talks about the immeasurable love of God. My favorite part is verse 18, in which Paul tells us that he prayed for the Ephesians to have the power of the Holy Spirit to grasp the fullness of God's love. It is *only* by the power of the Holy Spirit that we are able to comprehend the magnificent love of God! We can teach our children about God's love every single day, but without a move of the Holy Spirit within them, they will not be able to understand this amazing love. Therefore, *our most important job as parents* is to pray, to get on our knees on behalf of our children and pray that they will know the power of the Holy Spirit and will be secure in the great love of their Heavenly Father!

Journal

_____

_____

_____

_____

Journal

_____

_____

_____

_____

_____

_____

_____

_____

_____

_____

_____

_____

_____

_____

_____

_____

_____

_____

_____

_____

_____

_____

_____

_____

> How great is the love the Father has lavished on us, that we should be called children of God! And that is what we are!
>
> ~ 1 John 3:1

"Christianity is not primarily a moral code but a grace-laden mystery, it is not essentially a philosophy of love but a love affair; it is not keeping the rules with clenched fists but receiving a gift with open hands."
~ Brennan Manning

- Get a drink, pen, and your Bible. Find a comfortable place to sit and allow God to fill you with His love this morning!

- Psalm 100:4 " Enter his gates with thanksgiving…" Write three things that you are thankful for in your journal.

- Read Ephesians 3:14-21 and I John 4:7-21.

God Is Love

By: Kathryn Egly

In college, my English professor gave our class the assignment to write a term paper on a classic book. You can't have a more "classic" book than the Bible. I chose to write on the theme of love from the Bible, and it was the only time I actually enjoyed writing a college paper. I enjoyed it because the assignment forced me to dig into God's Word and discover what it said about His love. The more you study God's love, the more your heart is filled with His goodness and love!

The Creator of the universe loves you…exactly who you are, with all your faults and inadequacies—He thinks you are worthy of love!

Becoming a mom helped me understand God's love even more than before. Having children opens up a new kind of love: a sacrificial love. I had no idea I could love someone who requires so much of me. But that's when I began to see how much God loves me. He literally gave everything for me, even His life. I can see how He still loves me when I mess up because I love my children that way. I'm disappointed when they choose wrong because I want the very best for them. I hurt for them and with them, but my love for them doesn't change.

> How great is the love the Father has lavished on us, that we should be called children of God! And that is what we are! (1 John 3:1)

Though I understood love a little bit better after becoming a mother, the love I have for my children doesn't compare to the love God has for us. God's love transcends human love. God's love is unconditional—not based on His feelings or our actions. He doesn't love us because we're lovable or because we make Him feel good; He loves us because He is love.

Take a minute and learn from your children. Matthew 11:25 says, "At that time Jesus said, 'I praise you, Father, Lord of heaven and earth, because you have hidden these things from the wise and learned, and revealed them to little children.'"

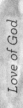

There are certain things our children understand that we do not. Children never turn down a gift. You hand them something, and they receive it immediately, with no questions asked! They don't wonder if they've earned it or if they deserve it. They just take it. We must learn from our children and receive God's love like that. It's a gift! Ephesians 2:8-9 tells us, "For it is by grace you have been saved, through faith—and this is not from yourselves, it is the gift of God— not by works, so that no one can boast."

God's not in love with a future version of you; He is in love with you just as you are. Receive His love today!

Questions to Ponder

· What is love according to 1 John 4:10?

· How did God show us His Love according to 1 John 4:9?

· How big is God's love according to Psalm 36:5?

Faith-Filled Ideas

If you are having a hard time accepting or understanding God's love, pray Ephesians 3:17-21 over yourself each morning. You may also want to read *The Ragamuffin Gospel* by Brennan Manning. Begin to search the Scriptures for what it says about love. Read each verse and let the truth of God's Word fill your heart with peace and love.

God so desperately wants you to rest in His love. He wants you to live your life knowing you are loved. Close your eyes and allow that to sink in. Imagine yourself curled up in your Father's lap. Listen to Him tell you that He loves you. Do that now. Close your eyes and bask in his love.

Now go about your day knowing you are loved and showing that love to your family.

Journal

_____

_____

_____

_____

_____

_____

_____

_____

_____

_____

_____

_____

Food for the Soul

Showing the love of God can be as simple as cooking a meal for someone. Whether it be inviting a friend over for dinner, making your husband and kids their favorite dish, or taking a meal to a family in their time of need, nothing conveys love more than a delicious, home-cooked meal. This meal is comforting and chock full of flavor, plus it has bacon! In our family, bacon is the sixth love language. My kids love this dish. They gobble it up every time and never leave a noodle to spare.

This recipe calls for either Brussels sprouts or asparagus, which I know can be pricey. As a one-income family of seven, we have a tight grocery budget. My tip is to wait and make this recipe when the ingredients go on sale, so you don't break the bank with just one meal. Buying produce in season is an easy way to keep your grocery bill low.

SUN-DRIED TOMATO BACON PASTA

By: Brandi Carson

Ingredients:

Olive oil

12-16 ounces thick sliced bacon, coarsely chopped

2-3 large cloves of garlic, minced

1 large yellow onion, cut in half, thinly sliced

1 8.5 ounce jar of sun-dried tomatoes in oil, julienne cut, drained

1 pound of asparagus, washed and cut into 2-inch pieces, or Brussels sprouts, washed and cut into even pieces by either halving or quartering, depending on the size of the individual sprout.

1 pound box spaghetti, penne, or linguine pasta

Salt and pepper to taste

Parmigiano Reggiano cheese, grated to sprinkle onto finished pasta

Directions:

1. While prepping your vegetables, bring a large pot of salted water to boil and preheat oven to 400 degrees.

2. Place either cut asparagus or Brussels sprouts on a sheet pan to be roasted. Generously drizzle with olive oil and season with salt and pepper.

3. Roast in oven for 10-15 minutes or until browned, turning occasionally.

4. Once water is at a boil, cook pasta as directed on box. Before draining pasta, scoop out two cups of the starchy pasta water and set aside for later use.

5. While vegetables are roasting and pasta is boiling, sauté bacon in a large, deep skillet on medium heat. Once bacon is crispy, use a slotted spoon to transfer it from the pan to a small bowl lined with paper towels to absorb extra oil. Set aside.

SUN-DRIED TOMATO BACON PASTA

<u>Directions (continued)</u>:

6. Remove bacon fat from skillet, leaving a few tablespoons in the pan with which to sauté onions and garlic.

7. Heat bacon fat back to medium heat, add minced garlic, and sauté for a few minutes until aromatic. Add sliced onions and continue sautéing until tender and soft. This will take 15-20 minutes.

8. Once onions are done, turn heat to medium-high heat and add sun-dried tomatoes, roasted asparagus, or Brussels sprouts, and half of the starchy cooking water. Sauté for a minute, stirring to combine. The starchy cooking water helps create a thicker "sauce" that coats the pasta. If after adding the water, the veggies seem dry and there doesn't seem to be enough liquid to coat the pasta, add remaining starchy cooking water. You don't want it to be runny or have too much liquid, just enough to create a nice coating to the vegetables. Salt and pepper generously to taste.

9. Lastly, add bacon. Place cooked pasta in a large serving bowl, top with vegetable and bacon mixture, and toss to combine. Sprinkle with Parmigiano Reggiano cheese and serve.

Love of God

~ Week Two ~

"And I pray that you, being rooted and established in love, may have power, together with all the Lord's holy people, to grasp how wide and long and high and deep is the love of Christ, and to know this love that surpasses knowledge—that you may be filled to the measure of the fullness of God." ~ Ephesians 3:17b-19

Hello Dearly Beloved Daughter of the King,

Oh, how my heart wishes to meet you in person—to share our prayers and our stories. My story may not have begun with a sweet, "Once upon a time;" but it does end with the delightful phrase, "She lived happily ever after."

You see, my childhood and teen years were filled with difficulty and sadness. My mother was an alcoholic who made many mistakes, and emotionally checked out on me when I was 10. She eventually left this world to go to the great beyond—to eternity, when I was only 20. As you can imagine, without a mother, I went on to make many mistakes myself as well. I have painful regrets and hurts, but one thing is for sure, I know what it is like to feel lost and alone, and I never, ever want to feel that way again.

The "she lived happily ever after" part of my story is by far my favorite—it's the life I get to live since I came to know Jesus Christ as my Savior, and began my journey with His great love leading the way. Though not perfect, and still filled with trials, my life is now defined by the unfathomable love of Jesus. His love is so wide and long and high and deep that the Bible says in Ephesians 3:17-19 that we have to pray to even understand it. That's an incredible love, my friend.

When I realized that we need to pray to even understand the *great* love of Jesus, I began to pray this little passage of Scripture each day and ask God to help me to understand this amazing love. I want to live life to the full just like the end of this passage says, "That you may be filled to the measure of the fullness of God."

Sweet one, are you perhaps like me, with a hard story to tell. Let the love of Jesus wash over you. Commit to praying each day, asking Jesus to help you to understand and live your life based on the firm foundation of His love. Then, sit back and watch that love begin to change you, from the inside out, and transform your life. Only the love of Jesus can do that.

Love,
Deb Weakly and the Help Club for Moms Team

> "*For we are so preciously loved by God that we cannot even comprehend it.*
>
> ~ *Julian of Norwich*

Mom Tips

"I am the vine; you are the branches. If you remain in me and I in you, you will bear much fruit..." ~ John 15:5

The Wise Woman Builds Her Spirit

- Download a Bible app on your phone. We recommend YouVersion or "The Daily Audio Bible." We learn about the love of God by reading and hearing His Word! Now you can listen while you are cleaning, exercising, doing laundry, cooking, or driving! Fill your spirit and learn about the love of Jesus!

- Go on a date with Jesus. Set aside a time where someone can watch your kids or when you will be alone. Grab a cup of coffee, park your car somewhere, go to a park and sit on a bench, or go somewhere in nature and just admire God's beauty. Talk to God like you would a friend. Try to picture Jesus sitting or walking beside you. This reminds us that God loves to spend time with us.

The Wise Woman Loves Her Husband

- Either make or buy a special treat for your husband. Place it in a brown paper bag with a sweet note or Scripture and give it to him before going to work. Be sure to give him a kiss as he leaves.

- Before your husband comes home from work, turn down the blankets on your bed and place a chocolate on his pillow with a note saying, "Can't wait to share this with you later." As he changes or sees your intentional invitation, be prepared to share some special time together.

The Wise Woman Loves Her Children

- Read with your children this week. Choose your child's favorite Bible story or storybook.

- Your children will learn about God's love by observing your Christ-like love for them! Work on being quick to listen, slow to speak, and slow to anger this week (James 1:19)!

The Wise Woman Cares For Her Home

- Plan what you are going to have for dinner by 9 a.m. every day this week. Try to utilize items you already have on hand to prepare family meals. Challenge yourself to think outside your regular meal rotation and use what is on your pantry shelves.

- Before the fall season sets in, get your kids to help you deep clean the car. Remove all those crumbs, crayons, wrappers, and whatever else is hiding under the seats. Finish with a new car freshner to refresh the scent.

> **"**And if God cares so wonderfully for wildflowers that are here today and thrown into the fire tomorrow, He will certainly care for you. **"**
>
> ~ Matthew 6:30 (NLT)

"The degree to which we worry about provision today is directly related to how much we believe we are loved and valued by our heavenly Father."
~ Joseph Prince

- Call your prayer partner for your 10-minute prayer call! Never underestimate the power of praying with a friend.

- It's time to meet with your good and loving Father. You can take a deep breath and relax because His character can be trusted! Close your eyes and invite Him into your space as you prepare to learn more about Him.

- Read Psalm 145. Write verse 9 in your journal.

God's Goodness~
A Foundation of My Faith

By: Mari Jo Mast

Did you know, what you believe about the goodness of God determines your future? Do you believe He is good? Your answer to this last question either establishes your heart in uncertainty or authority. What you perceive about God's character influences your ability to put your trust and faith in Him.

Here's the truth: according to God's Word, His goodness cannot be exaggerated!

In the Old and New Testament, we have many Scriptures supporting and revealing God's goodness. Nahum 1:7 (NLT) says, "The Lord is good, a strong refuge when trouble comes. He is close to those who trust in Him." In the Psalms, David speaks of His goodness over and over. Psalm 100:5 is just one example of many: "For the LORD is good and his love endures forever; his faithfulness continues through all generations."

As I was praying and meditating on this topic, God brought the concept of building a house to my mind. We all know and understand, in order to build a trustworthy home, the most important task at hand is to establish a solid foundation. Without it, the structure simply crumbles because there is nothing to support or hold the weight of it. Likewise, God's goodness is the foundation of our faith. Why would I trust in a God I don't know to be inherently good? It is impossible. Without true knowledge of God's character, our base is unstable, and we cannot build properly.

The Word says that Jesus is the cornerstone of our faith. It also says Jesus went about doing good. According to this truth, we can always count on Jesus. He is a solid foundation for our belief system.

I love what Bill Johnson, Senior Pastor of Bethel Church in Redding, California says: "Learn to get a theological cornerstone of God's goodness so firmly intact that the questions that are unanswered never undermine what you do know about His goodness."

In life, bad things happen that make us question if God is good. However, when our hearts are deeply rooted in the truth of the Word, which speaks of His goodness, we need not question God's motives, only trust, in times of deep sorrow or testing. We can then speak to our circumstances about our good God instead of speaking to God about our bad situation!

Understanding who God is at His core brings such hope and comfort. Psalm 27:13 (NLT) says, "I would have lost heart (hope) unless I had believed that I would see the goodness of God in the land of the living." Those who firmly believe in God's love, bring hope to others who are struggling—a hope that is contagious and anchored in His goodness.

Questions to Ponder

• What do you believe about God's character? Write down your thoughts.

• According to Psalm 145 verse 8 and 9, what is God like?

• Do your thoughts about God agree with what His Word says?

Faith-Filled Ideas

God is good even when things go badly. Building a firm foundation on this truth helps you weather the storms when they come. Look up Scriptures of His goodness and memorize them. Let them become the glue holding your belief system together. Speak them out in faith every day. Agree with God's Word; it doesn't lie. Below are some suggestions:

• **Psalm 145:8-9** (NLT) - The Lord is merciful and compassionate, slow to get angry and filled with unfailing love. The Lord is good to everyone. He showers compassion on all his creation.

• **Psalm 86:5** (NLT) - O Lord, you are so good, so ready to forgive, so full of unfailing love for all who ask for your help.

• **Psalm 34:8** (NLT) - Taste and see that the Lord is good. Oh, the joys of those who take refuge in Him.

• **Lamentations 3:25** (NLT) - The Lord is good to those who depend on him, to those who search for him.

• **Psalm 27:13** (NLT) - Yet I am confident I will see the Lord's goodness while I am here in the land of the living.

journal

_____

_____

_____

_____

_____

_____

_____

_____

Journal

> I have loved you with a love that lasts forever.
> I have kept on loving you with faithful love.
>
> ~ Jeremiah 31:3 (NIrV)

"It's not about finding ways to avoid God's judgment and feeling like a failure if you don't do everything perfectly. It's about fully experiencing God's love and letting it perfect you. It's not about being somebody you are not. It's about becoming who you really are."
~ Stormie Omartian

- Welcome to your time with the Lord! I pray it is peaceful, enlightening, and encouraging. Steal away in a quiet place and still your heart. Bring your Bible, journal, and a pen.

- Please read Zephaniah 3:17. Write this powerful verse in your journal or on an index card. Speak it with courage this week and try to memorize it.

God's Love Brings Freedom

By: Rachel Jones

My husband and I recently attended a charity ball. It was an incredible experience. The theme of the night was that God's love brings freedom and ultimately wins every battle. The speakers emphasized how lives are forever saved as a result of this love. After all, nothing is stronger and more resilient than God's love.

> Nothing can ever separate us from God's love. Neither death nor life, neither angels nor demons, neither our fears for today nor our worries about tomorrow—not even the powers of hell can separate us from God's love. (Romans 8:38 NLT)

This love cannot be vanquished, and it is relentless, pursuing us even in our sinful state, if we could only step out of ourselves and accept it.

Because of Christ's love, we have been redeemed from something weak to something wonderful. He is worthy, and He clothes us in His perfect worthiness when we accept Him and become His daughters. After we have become one with Him and He fills us with His Spirit, *He* brings complete freedom from our past, who we were, into our lives.

> For the Lord is the Spirit, and wherever the Spirit of the Lord is, there is freedom. (1 Corinthians 3:17 NLT)

Freedom is powerful. It is a gift. A treasure.

When we are blocking the Lord's love, whether due to guilt, anxiety, or fear, and not living in His complete freedom, we aren't living up to our full potential. Most importantly, we are not glorifying God's name. As I sat and listened to one particular speaker at the ball share her story, I was trembling from God's power. This woman revealed how for years she felt something missing in her life. Wow! She admitted that due to shame from an abortion and a divorce, her inability to fully accept God's love was hindering her as a mother and as a wife to her new husband.

You guys! She went on to powerfully proclaim Jesus Christ and His authority. She shared that one day He spoke to her, and her life was radically changed. God's love changed her life, as it did mine and most of yours! The love and grace of Jesus Christ are so completely freeing because they lead us to true worship, as we are forever grateful for His undeserved love. We are then focused on Him, not on our failings. Let me say that again....we are *not* focused on our failings! We have a calling higher than ourselves and an inheritance that is unfading—entirely built on His perfect love.

We also have the Almighty on our side fighting for us. As we daily battle with guilt and worry, He is there, offering His unconditional love. "Because he loves me," says the LORD, "I will rescue him; I will protect him, for he acknowledges my name. He will call upon me, and I will answer him; I will be with him in trouble, I will deliver him and honor him" (Psalm 91:14-15). God the Father is on our side, and what is more comforting than that?

The heart of our Father is revealed in those two verses from Psalms. Regardless of what we have done or what is going on around us currently, nothing can penetrate the protective shield and the freedom that God has placed around our spirits. When we trust that we are eternally secure because of God's great love and His ultimate triumph over evil, we can experience an unwavering serenity that transcends our circumstances.

Questions to Ponder

• Is there something from your past that is hindering you from accepting God's love?

• Who do you think God made you to be?

• What are some of your natural gifts and talents?

Write the answers to these questions in a journal. Pray about them and truly **ponder** them. At the Help Club for Moms, we believe it is very important to sit quietly before the Lord and not rush these kinds of important thoughts. It is in the stillness that God will often speak to you and reveal His plans for you.

Faith-Filled Ideas

Pick a night this week, or even thirty minutes over the weekend, to be alone. Ask your sweet husband to watch the kids, and allow yourself this time. Listen to the Big Daddy Weave song "Redeemed." https://www.youtube.com/watch?v=VzGAYNKDyIU .

If this song touches you like it has me, share it with that sweet husband of yours. Talk together about the "heavy chains" that you need to shake off. Grow together as a couple in the complete freedom of Christ.

journal

_____

_____

_____

_____

Journal

> "...neither death nor life, nor angels nor rulers, nor things present nor things to come,
> nor powers, nor height nor depth, nor anything else in all creation,
> will be able to ever separate us from the love of God.
> ~ Romans 8:37-39

"The greatest honor we can give Almighty God is to live gladly because of the knowledge of his love."
~ Julian of Norwich

- Grab your Bible and journal. Take a few moments to clear your mind of all the stuff of life. Say a prayer and ask God to help you soak in what He has for you today!

- Read Romans 8:37-39. Read it a couple of times until the words really sink in! Friend, nothing can separate us from the love of God!

Unboxing God's Love for You

By: Krystle Porter

Growing up, my view of God was similar to the relationship of a parent to a child. I am not quite sure where my thinking got skewed along the way, but to sum it up, I believed that when I was pleasing God, He was pleased with me and when I wasn't, He was a disappointed parent who shamed me for my bad behavior.

The thing about God's love is that we often do not understand it. We have never known it. Therefore, we can only grasp the things we know and try to turn it into what we think it should look like or feel like. Over the years, God has gently nudged my heart and expanded my thoughts on Him and His love. He has led me to verses like the one we just read:

> ...neither death nor life, nor angels nor rulers, nor things present nor things to come,
> nor powers, nor height nor depth, nor anything else in all creation, will be able to
> ever separate us from the love of God. (Romans 8:37-39)

Let me change some of that into a "mom-ified" version if I may:

...no matter how badly you have sinned, no matter if your home isn't perfect, no matter if you yelled at your kids for the tenth time today, no matter your children aren't always well mannered, no matter you forgot to have your devotion time today, no matter you responded rashly and harshly to your husband, no matter you woke-up on the wrong side of bed, no matter you had cereal for dinner, no matter you struggle with anxiety, no matter you struggle with depression, no matter you feel far from God, no matter the weight of your past, no matter your family dysfunction, no matter your difficult relationships, no matter your fallen-ness because you are human...nothing will ever separate you from the love of God!

Did you need to hear that today, mama? We can't understand this great love. We don't experience such unconditional beauty, but it is there, ready and waiting for us to consume and let it penetrate even the deepest and darkest places. If you are like me, and you have put God's love into a box of

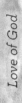

what you "know" love to be, would you do something today? Would you open up that box and let God out? His desire is to change everything you know! He wants us to be consumed with his love like a wild, burning fire and, friends, that cannot be put in a box!

> Beloved, let us love one another, for love is from God, and whoever loves has been born of God and knows God. Anyone who does not love does not know God, because God is love. (1 John 4:7-8)

Questions to Ponder

• Do feel far from God? Read Romans 8:37-39. Read it a couple of times until the words really sink in! Friend, *nothing* can separate us from the love of God! Take a few minutes to write down the things you believe are separating you from God's love. When you are done, hand them over to God and pray! Tell Him you know that *nothing* can separate you from His love, and ask Him to gently take those things from your mind. His desire is for you to know just how much He loves you without adding any limitations to it!

Faith-Filled Ideas

It is so hard to grasp God's great and unconditional love for us. We need to constantly be reminded! Write Romans 8:37-39 down on five index cards or pieces of paper. Put them in places that you frequently see throughout your home; beside the sink, your bathroom mirror, the dash of your car, or even inside the refrigerator (with hungry kids, that door is a revolving one!). Embrace this beautiful truth from God and never stop reminding yourself!

Journal

_____

_____

_____

_____

_____

_____

_____

_____

_____

_____

_____

_____

Holy Spirit
~ Week One ~

Hello Precious One,

In moments of desperation, do you ever speak out and say, "Come Holy Spirit?" These are powerful words, inviting the Spirit of Jesus into your atmosphere. He already lives in you, but it is a good thing to ask because we can never have too much of Him! It also makes us more aware that He is near and that He is our Helper.

The Holy Spirit is so very pleased when you are mindful of Him and desire to abide with Him because He also very much wants to spend time with you. He loves when you share every good or bad experience with Him. He is never bored by you. He is your friend and He truly cares!

As you study this week, make it a habit to call on Him. Stay in His sweet embrace all day long as you go about accomplishing the many tasks calling your name. Ask Him to fill you. His presence makes all things easier!

Love,
Mari Jo Mast and the Help Club for Moms Team

" Trying to do the Lord's work in your own strength is the most confusing, exhausting and tedious of all work.
But when you are filled with the Holy Spirit,
then the ministry of Jesus just flows out of you. "
~ Corrie Ten Boom

Mom Tips

"I am the vine; you are the branches. If you remain in me and I in you, you will bear much fruit..." ~ John 15:5

The Wise Woman Builds Her Spirit

- Would you like an easy way to organize your prayers? We love the idea of having a prayer binder. It's an easy way to keep all your prayers at your fingertips and will help you make a lifelong habit of prayer. For suggestions visit http://helpclubformoms.com/how-to-make-a-prayer-binder/.
- Play praise and worship music in your car this week while running errands. Dig deeper by listening to the Bible on CD.

The Wise Woman Loves Her Husband

- Acknowledge your husband and family as soon as they walk into the house by saying "hello" to them. This simple act let them know they matter to you. Make your home the place they desire to be because they are well-loved by their family. Teach your children to say hello to one another, too!
- If your husband is having a difficult week and is not himself, instead of being offended and hurt, take the opportunity to pray a blessing over him. Pray that God would flood your husband's heart with His love, peace, and grace. You are your husband's biggest prayer warrior. James 4:11 reminds us to not speak against one another.

The Wise Woman Loves Her Children

- Instead of catching your children being bad, catch them being good this week. Every time you see a child acting or behaving in a good and positive way, stop and praise them. Remember to say thank you.
- Take the time this week to learn about an unreached people group. www.Joshuaproject.net is a good resource. Find pictures and information about their culture and way of life. Pray for them and perhaps make a fun poster. Talk to your children about the importance of prayer, missions, and outreach (Mark 16:15, Matthew 28:19).

The Wise Woman Cares For Her Home

- Fall is the perfect time to make homemade snacks! Fruit strips, oatmeal raisin cookies, granola peanut butter balls, banana tortilla "sushi" roll ups, and frozen pudding pops are easy, healthy, and yummy snacks to have on hand.
- Before purchasing something for your home, visualize where it will go and if you have money for it in your budget. If it is a large purchase, try waiting at least 24 hours before making your final decision. Allow yourself to go without until the time is right.

> **"** Fathers, do not provoke your children to anger by the way you treat them. Rather, bring them up with the discipline and instruction that comes from the Lord. **"**
>
> ~ Ephesians 6:4 (NLT)

"I had been extra hard on Anne one day when she was small. The details have evaporated with the years. All, that is, except a small girl's tearful comment as I tucked her into bed, 'Mother, you make it so hard to be good!' Someone has said, 'A Christian is one who makes it easy to believe in Jesus.' Perhaps it could also be said, 'A good mother is one who makes it easy for a child to be good.'"

~ Ruth Bell Graham

- A big component of the Help Club for Moms is praying with a prayer partner for 10 minutes once a week. If you don't have a prayer partner, pray and ask God to bring her to you!! He is faithful and will provide!

- Start your day by interacting with Jesus. Grab your Bible, a journal, a pen, and something delicious to drink and go to the place where you meet with God. Ask the Holy Spirit to speak to you as you read His Word.

- Read Ephesians 6:1-4. Read the whole chapter if you have time.

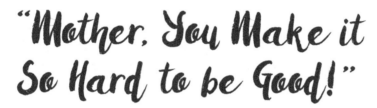

"Mother, You Make it So Hard to be Good!"

By: Deb Weakly

Not too long ago, my daughter Christie texted me a screenshot of this quote from Ruth Bell Graham with the caption "Saving for later." She and her husband are ready to begin their family, so she is pondering and praying about the type of mom she wants to become.

I felt myself getting emotional as I read the words, "Mother, you make it so hard to be good." When our children were young, I was a new believer and had no idea how to be a Christian mom. I read every book I could about how to raise Christian kids and, I am sad to say, not all of the advice was helpful. I remember reading that I needed to insist on first-time obedience from my kids and spank them each time they didn't obey. I began following this advice and now look back on those moments as some of the saddest of my life.

The nonstop punishments only seemed to make my children, particularly my daughter, more willful. I began crying out to the Lord for help. Each night after my children went to sleep, I knelt beside their beds and wept and prayed, asking God what I was doing wrong and begging Him to help me. I felt Him telling me to simply spend time with Him each day. I soon began the habit of a daily quiet time, reading my Bible and praying. I asked the Lord to wake me up a little earlier each day, and He always did. Each day I prayed for wisdom and the ability to see inside my children's hearts to discern what was really going on with them. You know what? God is so faithful; He showed me!

One day, I read the words of Ephesians 6:4 (NLT) and they rang in my heart.

> Fathers, do not provoke your children to anger by the way you treat them. Rather, bring them up with the discipline and instruction that comes from the Lord.

I began asking, "Am I embittering my children by over-disciplining? Could I be the cause of my children's continued bad behavior? Is my impatience and lack of grace a problem too?" Yes, yes, yes! All of the above was happening. I quickly saw how each day I was basically a drill sergeant in my home. It seemed like all I did was bark out orders and dole out discipline to my kids. This, in turn, made me feel as if I were a bad mom whose children's hearts were far away from her. I wanted to raise up Christian children for the Lord and have a happy home, but my home didn't feel so happy.

I remember a season when my daughter was little and she would come into my room at night after we put her to bed. By nighttime, I was so done with parenting that all I wanted to do was sleep. As you can imagine, I didn't react to this behavior very well. I even spanked her a few times for disobeying, and of course, that always made matters worse.

I began asking the Lord to show me what was really going on. Christie loved it when I put a shoe in the crack of her door to keep it open at night. For some reason, our air conditioner would maneuver the little sandal out of the door crack, and it would then close. She simply wanted me to put the sandal back and was even willing to endure a spanking if I could somehow fix the situation.

I prayed and asked God to help me be more patient. Soon, every time the shoe would come out and the door would close, I would fix it, but without anger. God was really helping me! I started to look at bedtime as more of a special bonding time with my children. The prayers helped me discern what was going on in my children's hearts, especially during the teen years.

Recently, Christie and I were talking about the shoe in the door ritual. She began to share with me the real motivation for coming into my bedroom and getting me to fix the problem. You see, my daughter's love language is acts of service, and it meant a lot to her for me to do that. When the shoe came out of the door crack, she felt like she wasn't taking care of what I had done for her. I know, that seems crazy, but who can completely understand the human heart except for God?

I am so grateful beyond words for the ever-present help of the Holy Spirit. What if I hadn't stopped and asked God for wisdom and help? I would have continued spanking and thereby causing my daughter to be distant. I would have missed the beautiful times spent in bed at night when my daughter's heart was open to me.

Dearest mama, does any of my story resonate with you? Do you have a child who seems to get into trouble, no matter what you do? Go to God and ask Him to tell you what's really going on. He will not disappoint! You are never alone in your parenting. You have the wonderful Holy Spirit, right inside of you, who will lead you in the way you should go.

Questions to Ponder

• Pray and ask God if there is anything you are doing to "embitter" your children. Maybe the bad behavior isn't all your child's fault. Ask God to show you new ways to parent and begin writing these answers down in your journal as they come to you. Then ask God to help you obey Him. Yes, we need to obey what God tells us to do; we sin when we don't. I think often of the convicting verse that says, "Remember, it is sin to know what you ought to do and then not do it" (James 4:17 NLT).

Ouch! God help me not to sin by what I know to do, but choose not to do!

Faith-Filled Ideas

Become a student of your child's heart and personality. Is she introverted or extroverted? Does she get worn out with too much activity? Does she need you to hold her close when she's upset instead of pulling away?

Begin a section in your journal in which you purposely pray for God to show you what you need to know about your child. Become an observer of your children and write down what God tells you. Ask Him for helpful books to help you understand your child as who He made him or her to be. I love the book *Discovering Your Children's Gifts* by Don and Katie Fortune.

If they are old enough, the "Myers Briggs" Personality Test is also a helpful tool. You can find it for free at http://www.humanmetrics.com/cgi-win/jtypes2.asp. You should take it too! It is so encouraging to see your child's strengths explained in a way that helps us understand where the rub in parenting that child comes from, and how to overcome these parenting hurdles with love.

journal

_____

_____

_____

_____

_____

_____

_____

_____

_____

_____

_____

_____

_____

_____

_____

_____

_____

_____

_____

> " Are you tired? Worn out? Burned out on religion? Come to me.
> Get away with me and you'll recover your life. I'll show you how to take a real rest.
> Walk with me and work with me—watch how I do it.
> Learn the unforced rhythms of grace. I won't lay anything heavy or ill-fitting on you.
> Keep company with me and you'll learn to live freely and lightly. "
>
> ~ Matthew 11:28-30 (MSG)

"If the Holy Spirit were to leave your ministry [your home] today, how long would it take you to notice?"

~ Francis Chan

- Today, the invitation from the Holy Spirit is to come to Him, and He will give you real rest. God invites us to walk with Him and to learn from Him. Choose, in this moment, to block out any distraction and keep company with Him so that your burden will be lightened.

- Open your Bible and read about God's Holy Spirit in John 14:15-21 and John 16:7-15. What do we know about why Jesus gave us His Spirit?

The Holy Spirit & Abiding Motherhood

By: Michelle Anthony

Motherhood is a commitment of epic proportions! As moms, we spend our days accomplishing a vast list of important and...not so important things. These tasks are time-consuming and taxing!

Consider the sheer volume of resources available to "help us" in our duties. There are books that deal with ADD, bedtime, discipline, defiance, curfew, complaining, bed-wetting, biting, finances, friends, fighting in the car, manners, media, potty training...you name it!

Someone once said that "in raising children, the days are long, but the years are short." As a young mom, I wondered, "Will I make it through this day alive and sane?" and yet, now as an empty-nester, I can't help but wonder how it all happened so fast!

Although necessary duties fill our days, there is something *spiritual* about our mothering that often gets lost in the mundane. What does the Bible say to us about "true help" from the One Jesus called the "Helper?" The Holy Spirit is the One who can help us capture a glimpse of eternity in the midst of the ordinary.

John 15: 1-5 tells us that Jesus is the Vine and we are the branches. This means that we find our power and strength, our nutrition and life source, from Him. We are told in verse 5 that apart from Him *we can do nothing*. In the chapters before and after John 15 (John 14:15-21 and John 16:7-15), we learn "how" to abide.

Jesus is telling His disciples that He is about to leave them but that He is not leaving them alone. Essentially, He's telling them that they *can't* do it alone! He tells them that He is sending the Holy Spirit (the Helper), and that it is through Him that they will be empowered to live the life He has imagined for them.

I can't tell you how many times I struggled through the day in my role as a mother "apart from the Vine." I foolishly tried to parent alone. And as a result, *I felt alone*. I felt weary. Anxious. And yet, because of His kindness, my Savior would lovingly beckon me...reminding me that I was not alone and that He was available for strength, perspective, and comfort.

It was in those moments that I stopped striving and simply would pray, "Holy Spirit, help me. Give me the strength and wisdom I need in this situation. Grant me Your peace and Your love so that I can have those things to give to my children. You have entrusted these children to me, but You have never asked me to parent them without *you*! Refresh me in the midst of chaos. Renew my mind and give me Your clarity. I worship You and abide in You alone."

Abiding in the power of the Holy Spirit is not something we do once; it's something we choose to do *continually*. As soon as we begin to come unraveled or sense that we are trying to muster out our motherhood in our strength is the very moment we must stop. Stop whatever we are doing or the thoughts that consume us and ask Him for help. It's something that will happen dozens or even hundreds of times in a day. And don't be afraid to bring your children in on this narrative. Allow them to see that mommy needs to go to God's Holy Spirit for all her needs. As you model abiding, your children will learn from an early age the importance of this discipline.

Questions to Ponder

• In what ways are you trying to "go it alone?" What circumstances or triggers cause you to disconnect from your source of strength in the Holy Spirit?

• Have you bought into the lie of "perfect parenting?" Are you drained and discouraged trying to impress everyone...including yourself?

• Identify some practices and/or people that will encourage your dependence upon the Holy Spirit both in the posture of your heart and the actions you implement.

Faith-Filled Ideas

Here are some ideas that helped me as a young mom turn the routine duties of parenting into a life that had a more spiritual perspective:

1. Determine to worry less and pray more.
  • Recognize that worry is an energy zapper!
  • Set aside time each day for a few minutes of quiet reflection in God's Word and time in prayer.
  • When a difficult situation arises, ask God's Holy Spirit for wisdom and strength before acting.
  • Write out prayers or verses and place them around your home for encouragement.
  • Pray with and for your child.

2. Abandon the idea of perfect parenting.
  • When you fail, ask for forgiveness. Model how your children should respond when they fail.
  • Dismiss the urge to impress everyone...including yourself!
  • Set realistic goals and communicate them to your family members.
  • Resist the "Super-Parent" lie...and ask for help!

3. Be involved with like-minded parents.
- Get or stay involved in a local church and "mom" groups.
- Meet neighbors with your same values to create play dates or outings.
- Take time for yourself to have "adult conversations"...guilt free!

Start putting these things into practice today! At the end of the day, you may still feel exhausted as you drop into bed, but you will know that you have invested in what really matters most in this life!

Journal

_____

_____

_____

_____

_____

_____

_____

_____

_____

_____

_____

_____

_____

_____

_____

_____

_____

_____

_____

_____

_____

> *Nevertheless, I tell you the truth: it is to your advantage that I go away, for if I do not go away, the Helper will not come to you. But if I go, I will send him to you.*
>
> ~ John 16:7 (ESV)

Holy Spirit

"There is a way to live a simple, joy-filled, peaceful life, and the key is learning how to be led by the Holy Spirit."
~ Joyce Meyer

- Get ready to meet with your Savior! He loves you more than you could ever know!

- Read Isaiah 11:2 and Romans 8:26. Be encouraged as you learn more about the Holy Spirit. He is a mighty Helper who is always with us!

The Holy Spirit Is Our Helper

By: Kristi Valentine

Sadness fills my heart thinking about Jesus permanently leaving the disciples in John 16:7. Instead of lamenting words, Jesus told them, "...it is to your advantage that I go away, for if I do not go away, the Helper will not come to you. But if I go, I will send him to you" John 16:7 (ESV).

Jesus called the Holy Spirit our "Helper," and He taught us that it is best to have the Holy Spirit come and be with us. Why? Who is the Holy Spirit? All throughout the Bible, we learn that the Holy Spirit helps us, is within us, and never leaves us.

- In John 14:26, Jesus declares that the Helper will teach us all things and remind us of the words of God.
- In Romans 8:26, we are so encouraged to learn that the Spirit helps us when we are weak and even teaches us how to pray.
- John 14:16 says that the Helper will be with us forever and dwells inside of us.
- Isaiah 11:2 comforts us by showing us that the Spirit of the Lord rests on us and gives us wisdom, understanding, counsel, might, knowledge, and fear of the Lord.
- Finally, Acts 1:8 boldly proclaims that the Holy Spirit gives us power!

Dear mamas, the Holy Spirit gives you all you need to be a great mom. Abide by the Holy Spirit! Walk with Him daily. He is always with you, and when you are so exhausted from serving your children all day (and night), He will help you in your weakness. Have you ever felt so wiped out that you can't even pray? The Bible says that the Spirit helps us to pray when we can't. I am in awe that He intercedes to God for us with "groanings too deep for words" (Romans 8:26 NASB). When I am too weak to cry for help, the Holy Spirit cries out to my Heavenly Father for me. My love for the Spirit is so strengthened, and my heart is so encouraged by this news.

How many times do we mamas yearn to know what is best for our children? What should we do when they are sick? How do we help them sleep? How do we teach them to love their siblings? Isaiah 11 says that the Spirit of the Lord gives us wisdom, understanding, counsel, might, and knowledge. We need to lean on the Holy Spirit because the very words of Jesus in John 14:26 (ESV) were, "The Helper, the Holy Spirit, whom the Father will send in My name, will teach you all things." Amazingly, Jesus didn't say "some" things. He meant that everything we need to know, as a mom, is available to us through His Holy Spirit, who lives in us!

Finally, the Bible says that we will receive power when the Spirit comes upon us (Acts 1). Mamas, even when the nights are long and sleepless, the children are needy, and nothing else gets done, we can cry out for the Spirit's power to help us. Jesus gave us the Holy Spirit as a precious, powerful gift. If we abide in Him, our Helper who never leaves us, we will be filled with heavenly power to be the loving, godly mama He calls us to be.

Questions to Ponder

- The Holy Spirit whispers to us in a "still, small voice" (1 Kings 19:12) and reveals God's will to us. He will tell you what to do when your child is sick or not sleeping. Can you hear Him? What can you do to hear Him more often?

- The Bible frequently declares the incredible attributes of the Holy Spirit. This helpful Open Bible webpage (https://www.openbible.info/topics/holy_spirit) is filled with beautiful Scriptures about who our Helper is. Read these verses and write in your journal the ones that speak to your heart.

Faith-Filled Ideas

Memorize Galatians 5:22-23 with your children:

> But the fruit of the Spirit is love, joy, peace, patience, kindness, goodness, faithfulness, gentleness, self-control; against such things there is no law.

If you search the internet for "fruit of the Spirit," there are fun printables of delicious strawberries, cherries, and bananas, labeled with each of the nine "fruit of the Spirit" character traits. Your children can color and cut them out and hang them on their walls. Teach your children that their lives can express this "fruit" to others because of the Holy Spirit who lives within them.

Journal

_____

_____

_____

_____

_____

_____

_____

_____

journal

Prayers for your Kids

this School Year

1. **Pray that your children will know that God is with them. He is their strength!** "Have I not commanded you? Be strong and courageous! Do not tremble or be dismayed, for the LORD your God is with you wherever you go" (Joshua 1:9 NASB).

2. **Pray that your children will listen to God's voice and follow in His ways.** "Your ears will hear a word behind you, "This is the way, walk in it," whenever you turn to the right or to the left" (Isaiah 30:21 NASB).

3. **Pray that your children will set an example for others in speech, conduct, love, faith, and purity.** "Let no one look down on your youthfulness, but rather in speech, conduct, love, faith, *and* purity, show yourself an example of those who believe" (1 Timothy 4:12 NASB).

4. **Pray that your children would be diligent and hard-working in their academics and in their study of God's word.** "Be diligent to present yourself approved to God as a workman who does not need to be ashamed, accurately handling the word of truth" (2 Timothy 2:15 NASB).

5. **Pray that your children will do justice, love kindness, and walk humbly with the Lord.** "He has told you, O man, what is good; and what does the LORD require of you but to do justice, to love kindness, and to walk humbly with your God" (Micah 6:8 NASB)?

6. **Pray that your children will do good to all around them, both those within your family and outside of it as well.** "So then, while we have opportunity, let us do good to all people, and especially to those who are of the household of the faith" (Galatians 6:10 NASB).

7. **Pray that your children will not choose to do wrong, but instead will overcome evil with good.** "Do not be overcome by evil, but overcome evil with good" (Romans 12:21 NASB).

8. **Pray that your children will love God with all their heart, soul, and mind and that they will love others well.** "And He said to him, " 'You shall love the Lord your God with all your heart, and with all your soul, and with all your mind.' This is the great and foremost commandment. The second is like it, 'You shall love your neighbor as yourself'" (Matthew 22:37-39 NASB).

9. **Pray that the Lord would complete the work that He is doing in your children and that you would be able to trust His timing.** "For I am confident of this very thing, that He who began a good work in you will perfect it until the day of Christ Jesus" (Philippians 1:6 NASB).

10. **Pray that your children will know, through the power of the Holy Spirit, to know how wide, long, high, and deep is the love of Christ for them.** "I pray that out of his glorious riches he may strengthen you with power through his Spirit in your inner being, so that Christ may dwell in your hearts through faith. And I pray that you, being rooted and established in love, may have power, together with all the Lord's holy people, to grasp how wide and long and high and deep is the love of Christ, and to know this love that surpasses knowledge—that you may be filled to the measure of all the fullness of God" (Ephesians 3:16-19).

Holy Spirit

~ Week Two ~

"God's love has been poured into our hearts through the Holy Spirit who has been given to us." ~ Romans 5:5 (ESV)

Dear Sister in Christ,

I have to admit something, I don't really understand the Holy Spirit. It seems the more I learn of Him, the less I grasp. I've felt insecure, wondering how I could lack understanding of the One who lives inside me. But, the Holy Spirit is teaching me that, as Christ followers, understanding Him is far less important than worshipping Him for His greatness and power! I marvel at the fact that He, the Spirit of the *Living God*, is living inside of me, empowering me! Just think about that for a moment; the Spirit that raised Jesus Christ from the dead is also *living in you!*

I want to be like the early believers in the book of Acts who didn't understand the Holy Spirit either, but prayed together and waited for Him; waited for Him to show His power, waited for Him to move. They surrendered in reverence to that which they couldn't fully comprehend. We, on the other hand, often get bored when we can't put a label on something or figure out how it works so we move onto something easier, or something we can control. Sisters, this cannot be! To be so enamored with the Holy Spirit, captivated by the mystery of His presence and work in us, will bring the joy, peace, and power we long for. This week, intentionally fix your eyes on *Him!* You are not alone; you have the power of Christ inside of you! Open up your heart to Him! Let yourself stand in awe of Him *because* you don't understand Him. The more He reveals Himself to me, the more I realize this is going to change my life completely, and my friend, I am pretty sure it will change yours as well!

Love,
Tara Davis and the Help Club for Moms Team

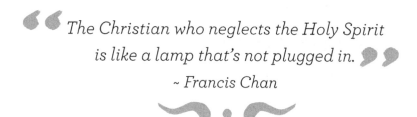

The Christian who neglects the Holy Spirit is like a lamp that's not plugged in.
~ *Francis Chan*

Mom Tips

"I am the vine; you are the branches. If you remain in me and I in you, you will bear much fruit..." ~ John 15:5

The Wise Woman Builds Her Spirit

- Do you want God's power in your life? Ask Him to fill you with the power of His Holy Spirit so you can be more like Jesus and walk in His wisdom.

- Continue to work on your Prayer Binder this week. The time you invest in this project is well worth it!

The Wise Woman Loves Her Husband

- Speak highly about your husband in front of others. Be his biggest cheerleader! Talk about his accomplishments and great qualities to someone. Practice the principle behind Ephesians 4:29 and "build others up."

- Spend 10 minutes every morning praying Scripture over your husband. Here are some suggestions:

  - Proverbs 18 - Listen without interruptions.
  - James 1:19 - Speak without accusing.
  - Proverbs 21:26 - Give without sparing.
  - Colossians 1:9 - Pray without ceasing.
  - Proverbs 17:1 Answer without arguing.
  - Ephesians 4:15 - Share without pretending.
  - Philippians 2:14 - Enjoy without complaint.
  - 1 Corinthians 13:7 - Trust without wavering.
  - Colossians 3:13 - Forgive without punishing.
  - Proverbs 13:12 - Promise without forgetting.

The Wise Woman Loves Her Children

- Write the Scriptures your children are memorizing on index cards. Using a ring, collect them for easy reference. Talk with your children about the importance of memorizing God's Word and hiding it in their hearts. The Holy Spirit will remind them of these Scriptures in the right season.

- Children love it when mom takes time out of her busyness to play with them! Devote at least 10 minutes per day this week to play with each of your children. Be silly and have fun! They may remember those 10 minutes for the rest of their lives!

The Wise Woman Cares For Her Home

- While folding laundry, pray for each individual in your home. Ask for them to know they belong to God and are dearly loved by Him, and for God to help them to be compassionate, kind, humble, gentle, and patient (Colossians 3:12).

- Pray over each room in your house. Ask for God's peace and presence to flow through your home.

> The LORD came and stood there, calling as at the other times, 'Samuel! Samuel!' Then Samuel said, 'Speak, for your servant is listening.'
>
> ~ 1 Samuel 3:10

"Your call will become clear as your mind is transformed by the reading of Scripture and the internal work of God's Spirit. The Lord never hides His will from us. In time, as you obey the call first to follow, your destiny will unfold before you. The difficulty will lie in keeping other concerns from diverting your attention."
~ Charles R. Swindoll

- Call your prayer partner for your 10-minute prayer call. If you are having continual difficulty connecting with your prayer partner, pray and ask God for wisdom about what to do. If you feel that she is no longer interested in praying together, call her and ask about it. She may have a good reason for being unable to pray. Always assume the best! If she says that she can't be your prayer partner right now, pray and ask God to bring you someone else. Be on the lookout for this new prayer partner. God will bring her to you!

- Welcome, friend. Grab your Bible, a pen, and something delicious to sip while you soak in the presence of your Savior! Pray, "Holy Spirit, come. Give me new insight and understanding today." Read 1 Samuel 3 in the Old Testament, and if you have time, read 1 Samuel, chapter 1.

- Highlight or underline any Scriptures that seem to stand out to you.

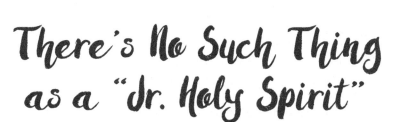

There's No Such Thing as a "Jr. Holy Spirit"

By: Rebekah Measmer

"No, you're too young." These familiar words have been uttered by many parents for thousands of generations. I know I have heard these words spoken to me, and I have proclaimed them to my own children a time or two. Even Jesus, the Son of God, was reprimanded by His parents for hanging out at the synagogue when He obviously should have been with His family at just 12 years old (Luke 2:41-52)! Too little. Too immature. Too inexperienced. The message is clear—and necessary in some situations. But are we encouraging freedom in the areas for which they are *not* too young, such as their walk with God?

During my childhood and "tween" years, I loved going to Sunday school and youth group. But praying and reading the Scriptures on my own? Not so much. That was something the adults did because they were more "spiritual" than myself. Did anyone tell me this? Of course not! Yet, I felt it keenly because Satan, the deceiver, put that thought in my mind and heart. Unfortunately, no one knew how I felt, so no one could correct my way of thinking. No one told me that I was *not* too young to hear from God through prayer or quiet time in His Word.

Holy Spirit ~ Week Two ~ Day Four

In the story of Samuel, the mighty prophet, we witness that God does speak to those who are little, immature, and inexperienced. Although Samuel was much younger than old Eli, God chose Samuel because of his heart. He didn't mind that the heart was in an awkward, youthful little body; He simply loved Samuel's soft heart toward Himself. You see, God can do amazing things with pure, eager, unquestioning hearts. And He values His littlest ones and cautions anyone against diminishing them.

> But Jesus said, "Let the children come to me. Don't stop them! For the Kingdom of Heaven belongs to those who are like these children." (Matthew 19:14 NLT)

Matthew 18:2-4 states that we must become like little children, possessing their humble, unwavering faith, in order to be accepted ourselves. Wow!

God desires childlike confidence—in children and adults alike. The Holy Spirit is the *same spirit* that raised Jesus from the dead and dwells in each of us who believe (Romans 8:11). On this topic, God is clear: there is no "junior Holy Spirit," and we must teach this to our children, reminding them of who they are. They *are* children of God, and they are *not* too little. They *are* loved by God, and He does *not* view them as immature. God *is* pleased with them *regardless* of their inexperience. And, they have the *same* Holy Spirit living and working inside each of them—just as Samuel, the boy who became a mighty prophet, did, which means that God hears and answers their prayers too!

Questions to Ponder

- Do I believe that the same Spirit that raised Christ from the dead is at work in me and in my children?

- Have I been encouraging and helping my children to read and learn God's Word for themselves, and have I verbally affirmed that God *does* speak to them through His Word, through worship songs/hymns, and through the wisdom of those around them—despite their youth?

Faith-Filled Ideas

Encourage your children to pause and listen for God's voice by practicing "being still" for 10-15 minutes several times each week (increase or decrease as their age and attention allows). Play soft worship music and have them quiet their bodies to listen, and teach them to say, "I'm listening, Jesus," or "Come Holy Spirit." After the allotted time is up, ask them "Did you hear Jesus speak to you?" allowing time for answers. Always encourage your children by saying, "Jesus loves you so much, and He sent His Helper, the Holy Spirit, to help you be kind and loving to others. Let's thank Him for our Helper and praise Him for loving us so much!" Pray and ask the Holy Spirit to fill you and guide these sweet conversations. You may be amazed at what God reveals to your sweet children through the repeated practice of listening for God's voice!

We all have the same Spirit and different spiritual gifts—no matter our age! Pray that the Holy Spirit would rest upon your home, and fill you, your spouse, and each of your children. Write a few of these Scriptures where your family will see them!

• 1 Timothy 4:12 (NLT) • Luke 10:21 • Romans 8:11 • 1 Corinthians 12:4

• 1 Corinthians 10:4 • 1 Corinthians 12:8-9, 13 • Ephesians 2:18

_____

_____

journal

> Nevertheless I tell you the truth:
> it is to your advantage that I go away, for if I do not go away,
> the Helper will not come to you. But if I go, I will send him to you.
>
> ~ John 16:7 (ESV)

Holy Spirit

"O Holy Spirit, descend plentifully into my heart. Enlighten the dark corners of this neglected dwelling and scatter there Thy cheerful beams."
~ Saint Augustine

- The Holy Spirit is your helper, and He wants to reveal to you a truth that you need for your day. So settle into your favorite spot, and see what the Lord has for you today through the power and presence of His Spirit!.

- Read John 16:1-15. Write verse 7 in your journal.

The Holy Spirit Is Your Helper

By: Carmen Brown

I will never forget the day that the beautiful truth of the power and nearness of the Holy Spirit was made more evident to me. It was the day that began a journey of discovering how close the presence and power of God is to us through His Holy Spirit. It has been life-changing to experience the Holy Spirit as the Helper!

I was watching the movie *The Gospel of John*, and as I watched the scene of the last supper, I felt overcome with sadness thinking about the disciples who had the presence of Jesus with them for three years and were about to be left alone without Him. I don't know why that hit me so hard, but the Lord used it to drive home the truth of the Holy Spirit in my life. Just as soon as that sadness came over me, I watched Jesus turn to his disciples and say, "Nevertheless I tell you the truth: it is to your advantage that I go away, for if I do not go away, the Helper will not come to you. But if I go, I will send him to you" (John 16:7 ESV).

Was it better for Jesus to leave them? That point was astonishing to me! I have so often longed for the presence of Jesus in my life, in my home, and in my struggles as a mom, wife, and woman of God. At that moment, the Lord showed me in a very tangible way that I *do* have Jesus' power and presence in my life through his Helper, the Holy Spirit. This understanding has led me to trust His guidance in my life and to seek Him when I need the truth of His Word in both difficult and joyful situations.

The other thing that my epiphany led me to understand is the nearness of the Lord and His desire to truly be Lord over my life. It has, as Saint Augustine states, "Enlighten the dark corners of this neglected dwelling and scattered there Thy cheerful beams." Those "cheerful beams" from the Holy Spirit have brought me hope and peace in the struggles that come. But they have also made me more aware of His presence in the mundane moments of life.

Are you struggling? Do you feel alone? Do you feel that God is far away? I want to leave you with these beautiful words from the gospel of John:

> If you love me, you will keep my commandments. And I will ask the Father, and he will give you another Helper to be with you forever, even the Spirit of truth, whom the world cannot receive, because it neither sees him nor knows him. You know him, for he dwells with you and will be in you. I will not leave you as orphans; I will come to you. But the Helper, the Holy Spirit, whom the Father will send in my name, he will teach you all things and bring to your remembrance all that I have said to you. (John 14:15-18, 26 ESV)

Seek Him today! Ask the Holy Spirit to fill your life and your home and to guide you into all truth. You are not alone! He is there to help you and give you wisdom and the ability to withstand any temptations or difficult situations. He is also there to strengthen you to love your family and to serve those who need you.

Questions to Ponder

• Do you long for a helper? Have you ever called on the Holy Spirit's presence in your life to help you and to fill you with peace or to give you a truth that you need? What is keeping you from asking for His presence? There is no condemnation for those who are in Christ, but if He is convicting you of any sin, then he is drawing you closer to Himself. Confess those sins to Him knowing that you are loved and cared for! Let Him carry your burdens!

Faith-Filled Ideas

Cry out to Him! He is there! He wants to be a close part of your life! Seek Him and the fruits of the Spirit in order to be a better mom and a stronger woman of God! He will not let you down! Ask Him right now to bring you a truth from the Scripture about a struggle or a worry that is on your heart. Take some time to listen for His guidance and write down your thoughts and the verses that come. Make this a practice in your life, and you will get better at hearing His voice and looking to Him for guidance!

journal

_____

_____

_____

_____

_____

_____

_____

_____

_____

journal

_____

_____

_____

_____

_____

_____

_____

_____

_____

_____

_____

_____

_____

_____

_____

_____

_____

_____

_____

_____

_____

_____

_____

_____

> "I will ask the Father, and He will give you another Helper,
> that He may be with you forever; that is the Spirit of truth,
> whom the world cannot receive, because it does not see him or know Him,
> but you know Him because He abides with you and will be in you.
> I will not leave you as orphans; I will come to you.
>
> ~ John 14:16-18 (NASB)

"Holy Spirit, You are welcome here. Come, flood this place and fill the atmosphere.
Your glory, God, is what our hearts long for, To be overcome by Your presence, Lord."
~ Kari Jobe, *Holy Spirit*

- Sweet sister, it's time to turn our focus from the demands of the day to find refreshing moments with our Savior! As you seek the Lord's presence, whisper or sing the words from Kari Jobe's song or find it on YouTube to help you invite the Holy Spirit into your midst. Come Holy Spirit!

The Power of the Holy Spirit

By: Rae-Ellen Sanders

At the very moment we repented of our sins and first asked Jesus into our hearts, true conversion happened, and the Holy Spirit began to dwell in us. His limitless power and wisdom came to live inside us, giving us the confidence that we are the children of God and have an eternal life in heaven. What an amazing gift!

Romans 8:14 tells us, "For all who are being led by the Spirit of God, these are sons of God." If you are a daughter of the King then you have access to the Holy Spirit!

The Holy Spirit is God. He is a member of the triune Godhead: Father, Son, and Holy Spirit. He has access to all wisdom and knowledge. Before Jesus left his bodily form on earth, he told His disciples in John 14:16-18 that they would not be alone and that he would send a Helper that would be with them forever. The Scripture goes on to say that He abides with us and will be in us. When we abide in Him, He leads us continually into truth, causing us to grow spiritually.

When the Holy Spirit comes to live inside of us, we have direct access to Him at any time and He also gives us spiritual gifts that God uses to help empower the body of Christ to accomplish the work of His Kingdom on this earth (1 Corinthians 12:1-11).

Jesus told his followers that when they received the Holy Spirit that they would be "clothed with power from on High" (Luke 24:49). This power changes a heart into a radical one, empowered with the ability to forgive, overlook offenses, to understand the spiritual realm, exemplify fierce courage, uncanny boldness, miracle power to heal sick and even raise the dead. Any Christian daring to invite the Spirit to empower them can experience the same spiritual gifts that were operating in the early church.

I love when Deb Weakly shares that we all have the same Holy Spirit—there is no Junior Holy Spirit—we all have the same measure of the Holy Spirit. She paints a picture of God pouring soup ladles of His Spirit into all of us. The same Holy Spirit who lived in Billy Graham and other amazing Christians lives inside of us. It's not that they had more of the Spirit; they just nurtured their relationships with God, and we can too! To what degree will you to allow the Holy Spirit to infuse you with His presence and His power? I pray a tremendous season of awakening and revival in your spirit and that you will live and move and have your being in Him (Acts 17:28).

Questions to Ponder

- Do you hunger for more in your Christian walk? Do you want to know more of Him and love Him more? This desire is your inner man yearning for more of the Holy Spirit. You aren't crying for something you don't have, but rather for more awareness and knowledge of what has already been given to you. Have you ever sought to have a relationship with the Holy Spirit? You can have the life-giving presence of the Holy Spirit in your life in an overflowing amount if you simply ask.

Faith-Filled Ideas

It's time to go deeper! Simply ask for the Holy Spirit to fall fresh on you. Give Him full access to your heart, soul, and life. Ask for the power of the Holy Spirit and the courage to exercise the spiritual gifts God has given you.

Journal

_____

_____

_____

_____

_____

_____

_____

_____

_____

_____

_____

_____

_____

_____

Food for the Soul

The Word of God is sweet and soothing to the soul, filling you up and comforting you. I love having my quiet time in the morning when I first wake up, hopefully before my five kiddos wake. I love to hear from the Lord and receive encouragement. It gives me a sweet start to my day and gets me ready for whatever craziness may lie ahead once all of my kids are up and raring to go.

To teach my kids that the Word of God is sweet and good, and to encourage a positive attitude toward God and their relationship with Him, I occasionally give them a sweet snack while having family devotion time. Reading the Bible becomes a special time my children look forward to and enjoy. As a bonus, their little mouths are occupied while they listen.

When I have time to make something extra special, I make kettle corn. My kids love kettle corn. Who am I kidding? I love it, too; it's crazy good! This combination of sweet and salty can't be beaten and keeps everyone pleasantly engaged while being fed God's delicious Word.

KETTLE CORN   By: Brandi Carson

Ingredients:

Olive oil

¼ cup coconut oil

⅓ cup white granulated sugar

½ cup popcorn kernels (I prefer white over yellow, they give a lighter pop)

1-2 tsp. salt

2-3 Tbsp. butter

Also needed: parchment paper and cooking spray

Directions:

1. Line your counter with two rows of parchment paper overlapping to give yourself a good area to dump your kettle corn onto to cool. Spray all of the parchment paper with a generous coat of cooking spray.

2. Heat oil in a large heavy bottom, nonstick cooking pot with the lid on.

3. When the oil is hot, test it by adding three kernels and wait until they pop.

4. In the meantime, mix your sugar and salt together and have them ready to go.

5. Once the tester kernels have popped, add remaining kernels, quickly add the sugar and salt mixture by sprinkling it evenly over the kernels and quickly cover with lid.

KETTLE CORN

<u>Directions (continued)</u>:

6. Shake the pan frequently, almost nonstop. You can take breaks every few seconds, then continue shaking. This is key to keep the sugars from burning. Shake, shake, swirl, shake, shake, swirl, is what I like to do to keep it mixed.

7. Repeat this until the popping dies down. If you can count to five between pops, it's done.

8. Quickly, with pot holders, pour the kettle corn onto prepared parchment paper and allow to cool.

9. Melt butter in a small dish in the microwave, then drizzle it over the kettle corn. Once it's cool enough to handle, mix well with your hands to distribute the butter.

10. It is ready to eat! If you store it in an airtight container it will last days, not that it will stick around that long!

Obedience
~ Week One ~

Dearest Mama,

When you hear the word "obedience," do you automatically think thoughts of being stifled without any free will, or does your heart relax a bit knowing that the Lord you obey is your guide who will never forsake you? I am praying it is the latter, for it is a joy to obey! And, it is in our obedience that we truly show Jesus our love for Him and our trust in Him.

As mothers, it is our heart's desire for our children to obey us. Our children's obedience to us results in a more peaceful and trusting home. In the same vein, our relationship with our Savior is more peaceful, and we feel more content when we obey Him. By trusting and leaning into Him, the Lord can guide and direct us toward our purpose. We can follow without fear, knowing He wants good things for us. After all, God's Word tells us blessings will come if we simply obey (Luke 11:28).

For the next two weeks as we study obedience, can I challenge you to submit one area of your mothering to the Lord? For me, I routinely struggle with my temper and getting frustrated easily toward my girls. In many of my morning quiet times, I invite the Lord into this space of hardship. Jesus does not want us to quietly struggle with being a mother! He wants us to obediently cry out to Him with reckless abandon! He is always listening and ready to come alongside us. I am praying for you, mama.

Love,
Rachel Jones and the Help Club For Moms Team

God is God. Because he is God, He is worthy of my trust and obedience. I will find rest nowhere but in His holy will that is unspeakably beyond my largest notions of what He is up to.
~ Elisabeth Elliot

Mom Tips

"I am the vine; you are the branches. If you remain in me and I in you, you will bear much fruit..." ~ John 15:5

The Wise Woman Builds Her Spirit

- Prayerfully consider fasting from a meal, caffeine, chocolate, or something you feel God asking you to give up this week. It could be for one meal, one day, or the whole week. Is there a question or concern that you need to give over to God? Use the practice of fasting to help you grow closer to the Lord and understand His plan for you. Use this time wisely by planning extra time with the Lord in Bible reading and prayer.

- Lay several open Bibles around your house to pick up for a quick read throughout the day as you're cleaning, cooking, and going about your day.

The Wise Woman Loves Her Husband

- When your husband asks you to do something this week, do it with a smile. A simple smile can show that you love to help and serve him.

- Be intentional about setting aside intimate time with your husband; schedule it in your week.

The Wise Woman Loves Her Children

- Make an "Awesome Jar" – A medium-sized jar in which to put notes you write, recording when you see a child being awesome, without being asked (opening a door for someone, cleaning, sharing or giving something away, etc). When the jar is full, take your children somewhere fun or let them pick a special place to go.

- We all want our children to have a servant's heart but there is no better way for them to learn than to see us serve. This week try to serve their hearts. Get up before your children and surprise them in their bed with a tasty drink. Take a few minutes to just spend time with them.

The Wise Woman Cares For Her Home

- Encourage someone today—right now. Call that friend who has been in the back of your mind. Send that email or letter that you have written about 10 times and never sent. Text someone you have not seen in church for a few weeks. Drop in and visit an elderly neighbor. There is someone in your life who needs to hear from you.

- Clean your dishwasher the natural way with this 2-step process; place a dishwasher-safe cup full of vinegar on the top rack, and run on the hottest setting. Next, sprinkle a handful of baking soda on the bottom of the dishwasher and run the washer again on hot cycle.

Now that you know these things, you will be blessed if you *do* them.

~ John 13:17

"If you know that God loves you, you should never question a directive from Him. It will always be right and best. When He gives you a directive, you are not just to observe it, discuss it, or debate it. You are to obey it."

~ Henry Blackaby

- Call your prayer partner for your 10-Minute prayer call! God is the one who has the power to work in your heart and the hearts of those you love. Prayer changes everything!

- Good morning sweet sister! God is calling you into His presence this morning. Bow your heart in surrender to Him today. He has a better plan for your life than any you could ever imagine. Follow Him!

- Write James 1:22 in your journal but check out the references throughout the study as well. God's Word shines truth over all!

Obedience

Discerning and Obeying the Will of God

By: Tara Davis

We are always searching for God's will for our lives, aren't we? So many of us love Him and desperately desire to follow Him. We search and ask God to show us His will, all the while remaining frozen in our places, just seeking. I am beginning to learn that discerning and obeying God's will for our lives requires only two simple things. First, we must stay intimately close to Him, hidden in His Word and in relationship with Him. Secondly, we must step out and act in the areas in which God prompts through His Word and the whispers of the Holy Spirit.

Sister, I have to tell you that if you are walking close to Jesus day by day, moment by moment, you will not step outside the will of God. If you are nestled closely to Him through studying His Word, through talking to Him and opening your heart to the voice of the Holy Spirit, your desires and motives will align with His and He will lead you one small step at a time. He will direct your path, and if you step off-course, He will redirect you right back to where He wants you to be. When you are intimately close to Him, you need not worry about discerning the will of God; He will reveal it to you!

But true obedience requires that we follow the promptings of the Lord as well. We must act (Matthew 7:21). It is a great deal easier to read our Bible, pray, and promise to follow Jesus wherever He leads than it is to actually take action and do what the Bible says. So many of us know God's Word, but His Word stops at our ears, never making its way into our hearts and out through our actions. Friends, we must become doers of the Word (James 1:22-25). We are called to let God's Word soak deep into our heart and to simply obey those words day after day (John 14:15).

I believe that Satan does not mind seeing us read our Bible, even discussing what we have learned with other believers, and then leaving satisfied that we have followed God for the day. What Satan hates is when we actually do what God's Word instructs us to do! Reading or hearing God's Word is simply not enough. Our deeds must follow as well (James 2:14-26). How often do you feel convicted, but then walk away and do nothing? We are oftentimes like the rich young ruler in Mark 10:17-27, who asked Jesus what is required to inherit eternal life. When Jesus replied that he must give up everything, the ruler could not bring himself to do it. He desired Jesus' message and felt conviction, but then walked away sad and did nothing.

What God desires for us is to run into His loving arms and actually follow Him in word and in deed. Friends, it is His kindness that leads us to repentance and it is His kindness that will lead to your obedience (Romans 2:4). You can follow Him and trust what He calls you to do because of His unfathomable love for you (Jeremiah 29:11). Take one step toward Him and then another until you are running in the direction of obedience, and what an adventure that will be! When our God-given conviction leads to action, joy and peace are sure to follow (Psalm 37:4).

Let me encourage you today, friend, lean in close to your Savior. Get to know Him through His Word and prayer. Learn about His character; the character He wants us to imitate. Walk in step with Him. Shed the rags of selfish desire and don the heavenly robes of a Christ-follower. And then act; do what the Bible commands, following the promptings of the Holy Spirit. Do not just vow to follow Christ in your heart, but follow by action as well. What a blessing it is to obey our Father.

Questions to Ponder
• How is God directing you today? If you are hearing God whisper, "follow me," do it! Wake up from your spiritual sleep and follow Him (Ephesians 5:14-17).

Faith-Filled Ideas
Read the story of Zacchaeus in Luke 19:1-10. Zacchaeus illustrates the wholehearted obedience that the Lord desires of us. When God called Zacchaeus to follow, he jumped into action with a passionate heart of love for the Lord. What is one area of your life in which God has been calling you to step out in obedience, but you have yet to take action? Pray and ask God to forgive you and show you how to follow His will with a heart of obedience this week.

journal

_____

_____

_____

_____

_____

_____

_____

_____

journal

Obedience ~ Week One ~ Day One

Obedience

> "Do not merely listen to the word, and so deceive yourselves. Do what it says. Anyone who listens to the word but does not do what it says is like someone who looks at his face in a mirror and, after looking at himself, goes away and immediately forgets what he looks like. But whoever looks intently into the perfect law that gives freedom, and continues in it—not forgetting what they have heard, but doing it—they will be blessed in what they do.
>
> ~ James 1:22-25

Obedience

"When you yield yourself in complete and wholehearted obedience to God, He can do great things through you."
~ Jim George

- Are you ready to spend time with your Jesus? He is always with us and available, but there is definitely something special about having a few moments to stop and focus on Him and His precious, amazing Word. Grab your Bible, something warm and delicious to drink, and your journal. Go to the place where you meet with God and ask Him to speak to you as you read His Word.

- Read James 1:1-27. This chapter is full of encouraging truths to help us persevere and obey.

Obedience Leads to Blessings

By: Deb Weakly

The other day, I was reading through James chapter one, and I was struck with an interesting thought—James must have been a dad because so much of that chapter could be applied to parenting. It's so interesting to picture the disciples as dads, and how they might have parented.

For instance, when you read chapter one, you see that many of the key points talk about what we need to know to be good parents: perseverance, keeping your joy when times get tough, wisdom, faith, believing God, living with less money (humble circumstances), trials, temptation (probably to lose it with your kids haha), being quick to listen, slow to speak and slow to become angry, and keeping a tight rein on our tongues.

However, my favorite point in this list is definitely the importance of obeying the Word of God.

As we read our key passage of Scripture today, God paints a picture of what it's like when we don't obey and also what it's like when we do.

God says when we read the Bible but don't do what it says, we are like a man who looks in the mirror and then walks away and forgets what he looks like. Obedience to the Word helps us to flow in the power of the Holy Spirit. As we stay close to Jesus, listen and do what He says, it's a whole lot easier to remember that we belong to Him and believe what He says about us is true. When we know we are not doing what He tells us, we feel guilty and condemned, which can lead to self-hatred and cause us to feel far away from Jesus.

Now for the good part. In verse 25, It says those who obey, "will be blessed in what they do." Don't we all want to be blessed, especially in our parenting? Of course, we do! Things will never be perfect on this earth, but "blessed" sure sounds like a good thing.

Many years ago, I remember a challenging season with teenagers in our home. It seemed as if every time I opened my Bible I kept coming across Ephesians 4:2.

"Be completely humble and gentle; be patient, bearing with one another in love."

Was God trying to tell me something?

At the time, I had a few little battles (let's call them moments) with my one of my teens, and I felt I was unable to reach her heart on a particular issue. After much prayer and meditation on this verse, I became convicted that God wanted me to act more humbly with my sweet daughter, and maybe the negative response I felt was more because of my attitude than hers. Maybe I was the one with the pride issue.

I began to pray, moment by moment for the Holy Spirit to help me to be patient, kind and humble. I tried to listen more and insert my opinions less. I asked the Lord to help me to assume the best intentions of my daughter more and more and began to call out the good things she was doing instead of always talking about what she was doing wrong.

Little by little, I felt my daughter's heart soften and turn to me. It wasn't always perfect, but I did keep trying and I am happy to say we made it through that season and came out as best friends. I treasure our deep connection and can't believe how blessed I am to be Christie's mom. Yes, I can honestly say God gives us great blessings when we obey!

How about you mama? Do you ever feel God tug at you when you read the Bible? Is He telling you to get rid of your critical spirit towards one of your children (Matthew 7:1-5)? Are you causing any of your children to feel exasperated by the way you discipline (Ephesians 6:4)?

Is the Lord telling you to give up some control of your teen and let her have the freedom to make some of her own choices, (and maybe even a few mistakes), while she is still under your roof? You might be terrified, but God is asking you to trust Him (Isaiah 41:10 and Matthew 6:34).

Whatever God may be telling you to do, it is always for your best; no matter how hard it may seem. If you have trouble obeying, remember what Jesus says in John 15:5, "I am the vine; you are the branches. If you remain in me and I in you, you will bear much fruit; apart from me you can do nothing." Jesus wants you to stay close to Him and ask for His help to obey. You are never alone.

Questions to Ponder

- In your journal, take a moment to read over the entries where God gave you a particular Scripture or piece of wisdom. Also, look over the Scriptures in your Bible you've underlined or highlighted. Do you notice a pattern? Write them down somewhere and begin to ask God if He is trying to tell you something through these verses. Write out a prayer to God asking Him for help to obey.

- Perhaps you have a particular child that you seem at odds with more than the others. Pray and ask God to show you this child's heart and what's really going on. He is so faithful and will show you! Write down what He tells you and start praying for wisdom in parenting your precious one.

Faith-Filled Ideas

Be intentional this week to spend one on one time with each one of your children. If they are little, playing a simple game together or jumping on the trampoline is always fun. We used to play *Uno* in bed with our kids right before they went to sleep.

Taking them out for a little ice cream or hot cocoa is also a great way to connect. If they are in high school, shopping is a great way to open up lines of communication, even if you don't spend a lot of money. Our trips to Goodwill hold many fond memories of fun times spent with my kids over the years.

Pray before your "date" with your child for God to bless your conversation and for you to enjoy one another's company. Ask God to help you understand your child even more and more as time progresses. And don't forget to give as many hugs as possible!

Journal

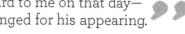

> Now there is in store for me the crown of righteousness,
> which the Lord, the righteous Judge, will award to me on that day—
> and not only to me, but also to all who have longed for his appearing.
>
> ~ 2 Timothy 4:8

"Love is not just a sentiment. Love is a great controlling passion and it always expresses itself in terms of obedience."
~ Martyn Lloyd-Jones

- Put on your crown. Look at your hands, dripping with the Lord's oil. Remember, today, that the Lord has adorned you with His favor and presented you in radiance to the world—a righteous woman. You are not the same. You are undoubtedly set apart.

- Read Jeremiah 1 and do a little research on the life of Jeremiah. Note how the Lord set him apart from the people around him, and how He marked him with righteousness and obedience.

Obedience

The Call of a Righteous Woman

By: Elise Turner

I remember, at seven years old, asking the Lord to live in me forever. I was on the porch swing of a tiny white house with my favorite old lady, Elsie, and some of her friends from the Good News Club. I had prayed the prayer of salvation many times before, but this time, I felt the Spirit within me grip my heart, pulling me fully and finally into an existence of righteousness and a desire to be obedient.

Since that day, I've struggled. I've wished the Lord had a different path for me. I've felt alone because of how the Lord set me apart. At 15 years old, my friends in the small town I was raised in were having sex and smoking marijuana. The Lord's protection kept me from those things, even though it meant spending most Friday nights as a teenager with my parents. Then and now, the Lord reminds me who He has called me to be, a woman untainted by the things of this world, and that identity continues to reposition me when I struggle. The Lord called me to obedience at seven years old. He's calling all of us now, no matter our ages or stages of life.

Our call of obedience is like the one of the weeping prophet, Jeremiah. The Lord told Him, "Before you were formed in your mother's womb I knew you, before you were born I set you apart; I appointed you as a prophet to the nations...I have put my words in your mouth" (Jeremiah 1:4-5). Set apart from the moment he was born, Jeremiah was a living testament to the Lord's favor and protection. Just like He did for Jeremiah, the Lord has set us apart from every falsely good thing this world has to offer because He has something better. He has marked us with righteousness so that we can be worthy carriers of His truth. Every day, we have the opportunity to demonstrate this righteousness: righteousness often comes through a choice between our flesh and the Spirit in us. When we let the Spirit win, we align with His will for us. We cannot help but be obedient.

Although the Lord calls us to obedience, it's His character and worthiness, not our own efforts, that sustain this way of life. He is the King of glory, enthroned and surrounded by angels singing, "Holy, Holy, Holy, is the Lord Almighty" (Isaiah 6:3a). His holiness is often what draws us into obedience. Like Isaiah, as we stand before the Lord in all his glory, we can't help but notice our sin and unworthiness. Isaiah responded to this picture of the Lord, "I am a man of unclean lips...and my eyes have seen the King..." (Isaiah 6:5). The Lord's response to Isaiah's sin was one of grace, as His angel told Isaiah, "See, this has touched your lips; your guilt is taken away and your sin atoned for" (Isaiah 6:7b).

Even more than His glory, His love and kindness leads us to obedience (Romans 2:4). A friend of mine told me about a time when she, like all of us, slipped so hard that she thought she was past redemption. For weeks, she carried guilt that drove her deeper into sin, until one of her darkest days, when she felt a physical embrace from the Lord strong enough to make her weep. He covered her in His love, and that moment inspired a life so driven by the law of love that its intentions and its fruits are now of the purest kind. Stories of life-long obedience like Jeremiah's are surely a testament to the worthiness of God. However, stories like my friend's, of redeemed righteousness and obedience, are equally demonstrative of His character.

Mothers and righteous women of God, set yourselves apart. The Lord has bathed us with water and anointed us with oil. He has wrapped us with fine linen and covered us with silk (Ezekiel 16:9-10). He has called us to righteousness, to obedience and full surrender, since before we were born.

Questions to Ponder
- How can you be obedient to God's call of righteousness on your life? What can you do to set yourself apart as a righteous mother and/or wife?

Faith-Filled Ideas
Look for the moments in which you can set yourself apart: when you want to scream at your kids, when it would be easy for you to join in on gossip about a woman in your circle, when you're tempted to complain to your kids about your husband.

Ask the Lord how a righteous woman would react to these situations. The Holy Spirit will guide you into obedience.

journal

_____

_____

_____

_____

_____

_____

_____

journal

When we seek to abide in Christ and obey His teaching, we find that God is faithful to guide us in every area of our lives. Jesus says in John 14:26 that "the Advocate, the Holy Spirit, whom the Father will send in my name, will teach you all things." In our culture, we are bombarded with so many different eating plans and styles to battle the effects of the standard American diet that it can be overwhelming. If this is a struggle for you, I encourage you to pray and ask God what is best for you and your family. He created you (Psalm 139:13), and He is the Great Physician (Psalm 103:2-3). He will lead you to the best nutrition for you and your family.

Overnight Oatmeal is a quick, easy, and healthy breakfast option. Prepare this the night before, and it's ready to go in the morning. You can also be creative with the toppings—the options are endless!

OVERNIGHT OATMEAL

By: Jennifer Valdois

Ingredients:

4 cups rice milk (or your favorite plant-based milk)

3 cups rolled oats

¼ cup chia seeds

1 teaspoon cinnamon

A dash of sea salt

Toppings:

1 banana

1 tablespoon chopped walnuts

Maple syrup

Directions:

1. In a mixing bowl, combine the rice milk and the oats.

2. Stir in the chia seeds, cinnamon, and a dash of salt.

3. Cover and chill in the refrigerator overnight. The oats will soften and be ready to serve in the morning,

4. Serve cold or warm up, if you'd rather. Top with pieces of banana, chopped walnuts, and maple syrup. This makes at least 4 servings, depending on your appetite. Portion any leftovers into individual serving containers and use the next day!

Obedience

~ Week Two ~

Dear Sweet Mama,

Have you ever heard the old hymn *Trust and Obey*? The lyrics are simple, and yet so profound: "Trust and obey, for there's no other way to be happy in Jesus, but to trust and obey." Oftentimes, we may feel unhappy in our circumstances or feel frustrated by the way life is, or isn't, working out. While the Bible does guarantee that life will be difficult (John 16:33), sometimes we make life more difficult or miserable for ourselves by doing things *our way* rather than *His way*.

Beginning with Adam and Eve in the Garden, the Bible is filled with stories of obedience, which always brought joy and blessing, and disobedience, where misery and separation from God inevitably followed. Friend, just as we are training our children to walk in obedience, our Heavenly Father desires our complete obedience, too! When I talk to my children about the importance of obedience, I describe it as a protective umbrella that keeps us and those around us safe. Stepping outside that protective covering through disobedience places each of us, or others, at risk. Therefore, my disobedient children must be disciplined because I love them and desire to protect them from future harm (Hebrews 12:6).

As you read through each of the obedience studies this week, pray and ask God if there are areas where you have stepped outside His protective covering through disobedience and are missing His blessing. Or perhaps you've been struggling with a child who continually pushes the boundaries of obedience, and you need a fresh dose of encouragement and wisdom. From one mom who is in the trenches with you—struggling, crying out, and needing Jesus to cover her own shortcomings each day; don't give up! Continue to press on toward the goal to win the prize that is in Christ Jesus, so that you may hear, "Well done, good and faithful servant" from your loving Father when your current struggles are a distant memory and you are rejoicing in your eternal paradise!

Blessings & Love,
Rebekah Measmer and the Help Club For Moms Team

" Don't you realize that you become the slave of whatever you choose to obey?
You can be a slave to sin, which leads to death,
or you can choose to obey God, which leads to righteous living. "

~ Romans 6:16 (NLT)

"I am the vine; you are the branches. If you remain in me and I in you, you will bear much fruit..." ~ John 15:5

The Wise Woman Builds Her Spirit

- Include your entire family in making homeless baggies with socks, gloves, toothbrush, toothpaste, and other toiletries. Plan to have these on hand in your car as you drive around town. Minister God's love by adding a pocket Bible.

- If you happen to have extra funds this month, offer it as a gift to the Lord by purchasing fast food gift cards. Have them on hand to give away when you see someone in need.

The Wise Woman Loves Her Husband

- If your husband prays before meals or at bedtime, or even brings your family to church, thank him for being the spiritual leader in your home.

- What is an area of disagreement you have been having with your husband? How can you die to yourself in this area and live in obedience to Christ this week?

The Wise Woman Loves Her Children

- Plan a fun outing with your kids this week. Go to a local pumpkin patch or an orchard.

- Teach your children the Ten Commandments, quiz them after dinner, and make sure to have a sweet reward when they can recite all 10.

The Wise Woman Cares For Her Home

- Clean or organize that one area or space you always avoid—a junk closet or drawer.

- As the leaves are falling, put on a jacket and grab a rake. It's good exercise to get outside and rake the leaves before they get overwhelming. Gather your kiddos to help and to jump in piles, then rake them up again. Remember to take pictures!

> For I am not ashamed of the gospel of Christ, for it is the power of God to salvation for everyone who believes, for the Jew first and also for the Greek. For in it the righteousness of God is revealed from faith to faith; as it is written, 'The just shall live by faith.'
>
> ~ Romans 1:16-18 (NKJV)

"Rest in this—it is His business to lead, command, impel, send, call or whatever you want to call it. It is your business to obey, follow, move, respond, or what have you."

~ Jim Elliott

- Pray with your prayer partner today. If you have trouble connecting, keep trying! This one habit will truly change your life and the life of your friend!

- Dear Sister, we all go through hardships in life...situations that take us by surprise, circumstances that keep us up at night with worry, fear and heartache. The Bible reassures us that God never leaves us or forsakes us and reminds us to walk in obedience. The deeper we dive into His Word—the greater He brings His purpose to the surface in our lives. Why not dive in together today! Find 1 Kings 8:57-58 in the NIV. Highlight it in your Bible and then write it down in your journal.

Obedience

The Wise Woman Obeys and Stays in Faith!

By: Rae-Ellen Sanders

Often, faith involves obedient action. The fishermen dropped their nets, Peter stepped out of the boat, the blind man washed in the pool, Rahab put a chord in her window and hid the spies, Ruth laid at the feet of Boaz, Abraham offered Isaac as the burnt offering, the wise men followed the star, Noah built the ark, Shadrach, Meshach, and Abednego walked into the furnace, and the list goes on! What is God asking you to do in faith?

My husband and I have been going through a season of standing in faith for provision as my husband obediently produces a film that God has called him to make without full investment. The world would say that our actions are irresponsible or even foolish. Sometimes, God calls us to do things even when we don't know how it's going to turn out, however, obedience is living by faith and not by sight (2 Corinthians 5:7).

We believe God honors those who obey, as indicated by the examples mentioned earlier. 1 Samuel 15:22 (NLT) says, "Obedience is better than sacrifice."

God is teaching me how simple it is to receive from Him during this season. I have learned to ask detailed questions because He has specific and exact answers to give. One of the most beautiful things about my relationship with the Lord is that I can seek Him anytime and find Him (Deuteronomy 4:29, Matthew 7:8).

He is not a far off, distant Savior but one who wants me to walk with Him as if I were Eve in the garden, seeking the plan He has for me and chatting all day long.

Although we have confidence that God is for us, there is an enemy who plants doubt and worry in our minds. I can't deny that I need to bind worry and remember God's call on my life to stay in the faith. Matthew 6:27 probes, "Can any one of you by worrying add a single hour to your life?" I've realized that during my trials and tribulations, worrying becomes pointless! Putting my faith in God, obeying what He says, and refusing to worry glorifies God and actually fights off the enemy.

Contend by trusting that God is with you all the time and has given you authority and victory in Jesus. Let me encourage you to trust that our Heavenly Father's love and power working for you is stronger than the devil's ability to harm you.

Believing is a big deal! Just look at the centurion soldier, Daniel, David, and Abraham.

> Yet he did not waver through unbelief regarding the promise of God, but was strengthened in his faith and gave glory to God, being fully persuaded that God had power to do what he had promised. This is why "it was credited to him as righteousness." (Romans 4:20-22)

> By faith Abraham, when called to go to a place he would later receive as his inheritance, obeyed and went, even though he did not know where he was going. (Hebrews 11:8)

We don't always know where God is directing us or for what purpose He is doing it. Sometimes, He reveals His plan, and sometimes we need to walk in faith. The good news is that Jesus has overcome the world! Jesus Himself said that anyone who loves Him will obey His teaching (John 14:23). Obeying Jesus and the Word of God is crucial in our Christian walk. To be overcomers, we need to trust and obey. Do you remember the old hymn, "Trust & Obey"? It says, *"Trust and obey for there is no other way to be happy in Jesus, but to trust and obey!"*

Questions to Ponder

• Do you believe God has a plan for your life?

• Do you believe He goes before you to prepare the way? God knows the plans He has for us. He is a God of the future, not just the past: He goes before us and prepares the way. In Genesis 28:15, God declares, "I am with you and I will watch over you wherever you go...I will not leave you until I have done what I have promised you."

• Do you have promises from Scripture that you cling to? God's promises are meant to encourage us in the day of trial; we are meant to treasure them and store them up. Read Isaiah 41:10, Psalm 18:32, and Romans 8:28. Find more verses that encourage you to obey and write them in your journal. Be tenacious for God's promises and be a woman who *obeys* and believes God for *big* things!

Faith-Filled Ideas

The Bible is full of stories of men and women of great faith that obeyed and were rewarded for their faith and obedience. Many great Christians like Jim Elliott, Corrie Ten Boom, Hudson Taylor, George Mueller, Amy Carmichael, and more have trusted God with their very lives and obeyed God's call. Their courageous faith has been written down in history for us to follow. Read the stories of these heroes of faith to your children. They will inspire you to have great faith, to obey regardless of circumstances, and not worry.

journal

> ❝ The boundary lines have fallen for me in pleasant places;
> surely I have a delightful inheritance. ❞
>
> ~ Psalm 16:6

"I'm beginning to see these boundary lines were meant for me so that I could find all the treasures hidden inside a holy God."
~ Sara Evans, *My Joy to Love*

- Enjoy a moment of quiet contemplation. Close your eyes, breathe deeply, and listen to Sara Evans' song "My Joy to Love." Allow the Spirit to restore your strength through this time of resting with your good Father. When you're ready, let's get into today's devotion.

- Read Deuteronomy 5:32-33, and John 14:15-31

Joyful Obedience

By: Brynne Gluch

Some may call me crazy, but even as a mom to toddlers, I want a puppy. I spend all my free time looking at designer dogs online. What has felt like hundreds of hours of research has led me to a few conclusions:

1. If you want a designer dog, you might need to start a side business to pay for it, especially if the dog's name begins with "teacup" or ends in "poo" or "oodle."

2. If you want to have your dog graduate from an obedience program before you bring it home, your kids can forget about your contribution to their college tuition.

3. While I may never bring home the obedience-trained designer puppy of my dreams, I have received revelation about the *cost* and *value* of obedience training.

I had a powerful will and rebellious tendencies as a young person. I saw rules as a form of control and rejected the very thought of being controlled. As it happens, I have a completely different perspective now that I am a mother myself. I see the rules I put in place for my family as a boundary fence around my most treasured loved ones for their protection and preservation. For example, after seeing police outside our house, my husband asked us to stay in the car while he checked it out. My daughter disregarded his boundary line, bolting out of the car after him. My heart sank. All was well, but while watching a special ops squad fall into position at a hand signal on TV later that evening, I yearned for my children to be obedient. Firstly, so I could keep them safe. And secondly, because that would look so cool. I've got to think that's how God feels about me.

Author Danny Silk writes, "Submission is not synonymous with demanding dominance over another person." Understanding this requires a perspective shift if we have an opinion of God as a controlling Father. The good news of the gospel is His grace! The juxtaposition of our two readings today shows us that we no longer have to earn our salvation.

The most radical example of obedience in the Bible is Jesus' willingness to endure death on the cross on our behalf. Leading up to the crucifixion, Christ said "I will not say much more to you, for the prince of this world is coming. He has no hold over me, but he comes so that the world may learn that I love the Father and do exactly what my Father has commanded me" (John 14:30). Jesus models for us that our obedience to the Father is a choice, but in choosing to obey Him, we are professing our love and God's Lordship over our lives. We don't have to worry about doing it wrong or not doing enough because Jesus paid it all for us on the cross. And in return, it is our joy to love and obey.

Questions to Ponder

1. Search your heart
   - What areas are you trying to take things under your control?
   - Are you walking outside the boundary lines God has set to protect you?
   - What is the "fruit" of that area of your life?

2. Isaiah 9:7a (NASB) declares: "There will be no end to the increase of His government or of peace..." Ask God for help answering the following question:
   - If the kingdom of heaven is full of peace, how can I govern peace in my home?
   - Are there areas of my parenting that are motivated by fear?

3. Read Matthew 20:25-28. Ask God for help in answering the following question:
   - How can I adjust my parenting style to reflect the type of authority modeled by Jesus?

Faith-Filled Ideas

Read this quote by C.S. Lewis and write your heart's response in your journal:

> [To have Faith in Christ] means, of course, trying to do all that He says. There would be no sense in saying you trusted a person if you would not take his advice. Thus, if you have really handed yourself over to Him, it must follow that you are trying to obey Him. But trying in a new way, a less worried way. Not doing these things in order to be saved, but because He has begun to save you already. Not hoping to get to Heaven as a reward for your actions, but inevitably wanting to act in a certain way because a first faint gleam of Heaven is already inside you.

Read your response to your kids. They will learn to obey you, as you model to them your obedience to your Father!

journal

_____

_____

_____

_____

_____

_____

_____

journal

Obedience

If you love me, you will keep my commandments.

~ John 14:15 (ESV)

"I have been crucified with Christ.
It is no longer I who live, but Christ who lives in me.
And the life I now live in the flesh I live by faith in the Son of God,
who loved me and gave himself for me.

~ Galatians 2:20 (ESV)

"The moment I chose to obey is the defining moment of my life."
~ Tricia Goyer

- Set aside some time to invite God into your dreaming and planning for the days ahead. He will tell you mysteries you do not know as you start walking and talking with Him.

- Here are some items to pray for today:

  1. Ask God to show you what ideas He has for you to follow through with the rest of this year. What plans does He have for your family? What ministry opportunities should you be involved in? What creative one-on-ones with your kiddos does He have on His heart? What things should you let go of that aren't essential to your relationship with Him?

  2. Ask God to show you the difference between good, better, and best.

  3. Ask Him to show you if He is your first love, do your daily actions reflect that you're dependent on Him?

- Read Genesis 6 in your Bible.

Following through with God's Plans

By: Jennifer Kindle

In just a couple of months, a new year is on its way with an invitation for new resolutions. But before you scribble resolves in your planner, let's look back at the beginning.

> But Noah found favor in the eyes of the Lord...Noah was a righteous man, blameless in his generation. Noah walked with God. Noah did this; he did all that God commanded him. (Genesis 6:8,9 and 22 ESV)

I doubt that Noah sat around dreaming up what he could do for God, but I do believe as Noah walked with God, God whispered "unrealistic" dreams as well as tiny steps of faithfulness into Noah's heart. As Noah said yes to God's big picture command to build an ark, his bravery to trust in God grew, his faith to believe and take Him at his word swelled, and each act of obedience created a legacy of walking blamelessly. Rather than planning out his own dreams, God's ideas were birthed in the heart of Noah, who willingly obeyed, and who was commended for his faith.

I'm a dreamer, maybe you are too. Perhaps you have unique ideas swarming around in your heart this very moment as you've been thinking about finishing this year strong, I encourage you to invite God into your dreaming. He has unique ideas that He planned for you to do, just as He had plans for Noah's life. As you listen to the heart of your Father, as you abide and hear His heart through Scripture, as you say yes to obedience, He will tell you all kinds of mysteries concerning you. He may put unrealistic dreams into your heart, as well as tiny steps of faithfulness for each day.

How can we know God's heart concerning us unless we are abiding in Him? It's in the abiding where He breathes His heart's desires into us and strengthens us to obey. Time spent with the Father changes who we are, how we think, and how we want to spend our time. As we walk with God, we can be sure our plans and desires are inspired by Him.

He is ready to impart his plans for us as we choose to abide. Are you ready to walk with Him and hear His heart? Are you ready to trust Him to grow your faith as you obey?

As the days went on for Noah, building that ark, he was able to follow through with God's ideas as he kept abiding. Your abiding will stir up God's desires in you, and you will bravely resolve to obey regardless of the setbacks and discouraging days. Life will happen, hard days will come, but you will keep abiding, and on days when you feel like quitting, you will keep pressing into Christ and walking out His desires as an act of obedience. Even when you don't feel like it, you will obey because you know without a doubt that what you're called to do is straight from the heart of your Father.

You will resolve to walk righteously and blamelessly in submission to His Word whether you feel like it or not because your confidence in Christ has swelled with so much bravery that you literally believe every single thing God has whispered into your heart.

Keep abiding, sister, it's out of the overflow of that abiding that Christ lives through us.

Questions to Ponder

- Have you been abiding so close that you daily hear God's commands for you?
- Have you been making your own plans, or following God's plans?
- How can you carve out alone time with Christ?
- How can you abide even in the hurried busy of each day?
- Do you quit when you feel overwhelmed, or do you follow through regardless of your emotions?
- Are you confident that everything you're doing is from the heart of God?

Faith-Filled Ideas

Make a list of all the activities you spend your time on that don't draw you closer to Christ.

Make a list of activities that help you know the heart of God.

Make a plan to do more of what helps you abide, and less of what doesn't.

Practice talking to God as you go about your daily tasks, seeking His heart concerning laundry, dishes, serving your family, and your attitude.

Practice taking a daily walk, literally, go for a walk and talk to God. Tell Him what you notice in nature, ask Him to speak to you through it, ask for His heart concerning your day.

Obedience

journal

Obedience

Obedience ~ Week Two ~ Day Six

Journal

Worship

~ Week One ~

"Come, let us bow down in worship, let us kneel before the Lord our Maker. " ~ Psalm 95:6

Dear Sweet Mama,

Have you ever stumbled upon a new truth in your Bible that surprised you? God's Word is full of amazing accounts of how God has worked throughout history that continue to inspire believers today. And because the Bible is "alive and active" (Hebrews 4:12), the Holy Spirit can illuminate a Scripture or passage right from the pages to your understanding. Something familiar might suddenly have new meaning, or as happened for me with the Scripture below, you may discover a passage for the first time that *wows* you! While researching on the topic of worship for *The Wise Woman Abides,* this passage in 2 Chronicles became a new favorite:

> Jehoshaphat bowed down with his face to the ground, and all the people of Judah and Jerusalem fell down in worship before the Lord. After consulting the people, Jehoshaphat appointed men to sing to the Lord and to praise him for the splendor of his Holiness as they went out at the head of the army, saying: "Give thanks to the Lord, for his love endures forever." As they began to sing and praise, the Lord set ambushes against the men of Ammon and Moab and Mount Seir who were invading Judah, and they were defeated. (2 Chronicles 20:18, 21-22)

Worship is a conduit through which God's power flows. When facing an enemy who is coming against you, do what King Jehoshaphat did: he fell on his face before the Lord and worshipped. When you are fighting a battle that is bigger than yourself, bowing or kneeling down in prayer is a strategic position for those who know that God has already overcome. The King of Judah humbly led his people in worship during battle, and the result was a divine and miraculous victory!

While the people of Judah and Jerusalem were singing and praising God, He was fighting for them! God's principles never change. If you spend your life singing to and praising the Lord, God will be your warrior. I'm praying the next two weeks will inspire you to worship instead of worry, so that you will encounter God in a new, victorious way!

Never gonna stop singing,
Rae-Ellen Sanders and the Help Club for Moms Team

We need to discover all over again that worship is natural to the Christian,
as it was to the godly Israelites who wrote the psalms,
and that the habit of celebrating the greatness and graciousness
of God yields an endless flow of thankfulness, joy, and zeal.

~ J.I. Packer

Mom Tips

*"I am the vine; you are the branches. If you remain
in me and I in you, you will bear much fruit..."* ~ John 15:5

The Wise Woman Builds Her Spirit

- Start each day with a grateful heart. Write down in your journal five things for which you feel grateful everyday this week. Write Psalm 119:105 on an index card and keep it in a place where you can see it easily. Try to memorize the verse by the end of the week.

- Make a "quiet time basket." Get a simple basket and stock it with your Bible, journal, a pen, candle with matches, and notecards (for writing a friend an encouraging note). If you have small children in the home, keep your supplies safe by storing the basket where little hands can't reach.

The Wise Woman Loves Her Husband

- Praise God for your husband this week! Think of all the ways God made him special and unique (and be sure to share those things with your husband too).

- Pray that God will open up doors for opportunities for you and your husband to worship and serve God together. A married couple serving the Lord together is powerful!

The Wise Woman Loves Her Children

- Instead of one person praying before your meals this week, involve the entire family. Take turns thanking God for your day in a "popcorn" style prayer. This helps your children make the habit of talking to God about what brings them joy.

- Sing songs to your children or with your children before bedtime. These last words will soothe them before going to sleep. *Wee Sing* has many old favorites in hymnals just for little eyes to read and sing.

The Wise Woman Cares For Her Home

- Set a timer for 5 to 15 minutes and declutter that problem area you avoid looking at. Throw away the trash, put away the things that don't belong, and give away what you aren't using anymore. Make a goal to declutter the problem areas in your home two or three times a week.

- Fill your sink with soapy water and hand wash dishes with your kids. Be sure to make extra bubbles and have an extra good time!

> 66 My flesh and my heart may fail,
> but God is the strength of my heart and my portion forever. 99
>
> ~ Psalm 73:26

"To worship God is to admit that we are entirely contrary to Him and that He is willing to make us like Himself."
  ~ Brother Lawrence

- Remember to call your prayer partner today! Keep it quick, and keep praying for each other throughout the week.

- Dear mama, please quiet your heart before the Lord. Go someplace in your home where you won't be distracted or interrupted and have an amazing time with your Creator.

- Read John 4:21-24 in your Bible. Write these verses down in your journal and ponder them for a few moments. Are you truly worshipping Jesus in spirit and in truth?

Worshipping God through the Exhaustion

By: Rachel Jones

Have you searched your heart lately to find Jesus? Is He still there, or has He gotten pushed aside due to life's stresses and busyness? I am in a season where I attend church with my family, but I end up leaving the sanctuary multiple times with my baby, and my mind is nowhere near a state of worship. It is hard. Often, it doesn't seem worth it.

However, no matter the season we are in, worship is essential to our spiritual health and growth. Humans were made to worship and glorify God. In Isaiah 43:7 this is what God says about us, His people, "Everyone who is called by my name, whom I created for my glory." That glory He is referring to is bestowed upon Him through our worship.

It is so important to remember that God is gracious. Even if you only have a little to offer, He will take that and mold you to be more like Him. James 4:8 says, "Draw near to God, and He will draw near to you." God knows your heart, and He sees your tired eyes. But He also wants to be at the center of your life. We cannot let our full schedules or lack of sleep become a scapegoat for not turning to Jesus in worship. He expects, and deserves, our best!

God does amazing work when we come to Him in complete surrender and worship, holding nothing back. Throughout this season of motherhood, I have often turned to Jesus daily to get through my days, whispering His name to myself. I have learned that when I get to the end of myself, that is the start of Him! I love this verse in Proverbs 27:7, "He who is full loathes honey from the comb, but to the hungry even what is bitter tastes sweet"

When we are "full," or clueless about our state of need, or too focused on how tired we are or how difficult our day was, we miss out on the sweetness of God's sustenance for our souls. God can make the bitter and hard things in our life seem sweet and worthwhile when we turn to Him. He will gladly take our small crumbs of worship if they come from a pure place in our hearts.

Attending church might be hard. Being a part of a small group might be a thing of the past. But you are reading this Bible study, aren't you? That is a start! God sees you, mama! Now, let's worship Him together. Something I have been doing lately, and which doesn't take too long, is praying God's Word back to Him. Praying His Scriptures out loud in adoration is the ultimate way to glorify God. This act of worship has shifted my heart to believe God is who He says He is. In the times of complete exhaustion, remember these truths mamas: God is in control, He is Almighty, He is the beginning and the end, the lover of your soul, and the binder of the brokenhearted. Even when we have not made time for Him, He has not forgotten about us!

Questions to Ponder

• Please write these down in your journal and pray about them.
   1. Do you notice a difference in your life when you haven't made time to worship the Lord? How does it affect you as a mom?
   2. Contrast the above question to this one: what kind of mom are you when you have made the time to worship the Lord?

Faith-Filled Ideas

I would love to challenge you to take some time over the next few days to pray Scripture to our God in adoration and worship. Typically, I pray these verses out loud and spend some time thinking about them. It is truly amazing how powerful reading Scripture out loud is! Here are some wonderful verses with which to start:

   • Isaiah 6:3   • Psalm 29:2   • Psalm 33:8   • Psalm 99:5   • 1 Samuel 2:1-2   • Revelation 5:9-13

Journal

_____

_____

_____

_____

_____

_____

_____

_____

_____

journal

_____

_____

_____

_____

_____

_____

_____

_____

_____

_____

_____

_____

_____

_____

_____

_____

_____

_____

_____

_____

_____

_____

Worship

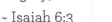 Holy, holy, holy is the LORD Almighty; the whole earth is full of his glory.

~ Isaiah 6:3

"Turn your eyes upon Jesus,
Look full in His wonderful face.
And the things of earth will grow strangely dim,
In the light of His glory and grace."
~ Helen Howarth Lemmel

- Make a warm drink, grab your book and a journal, and find a comfortable place to have your quiet time. Make yourself cozy, take a few deep breaths, and ask God to bless your study today.

- Read Isaiah 55:8-9, Joshua 1:9, and Romans 8:28. Reflect on God's loving-kindness and faithfulness.

Focusing on Truth

By: Heather Doolittle

Have you ever sat in a room (or looked at a social media page) full of people who seemed to have it all together, and thought how different they are from you and that surely no one else has the same struggles you do? I have, plenty of times. That is the result of shame: the ugly, hidden feeling that tears apart our relationships, preventing us from reaching out to new friends or sharing our hearts with old ones. It pushes us to strive to be something we're not, out of fear that who we really are is not good enough.

The worst part about shame is that it tends to be rooted in fact. I started following Jesus halfway through college, and so I had a few years of poor decisions with which to reconcile. I spent the better part of a decade circling back to that place and seeking healing and forgiveness for the distant past. For a long time, I didn't even realize I was stuck in such a toxic cycle. Beating myself up seemed necessary to atone for my sins, but that is only false humility, which is the opposite of what God wants from us. I was focused more on myself than on God, which left me shamefully aware of my inadequacies, constantly reliving the pain of my past choices and experiences. I thought I was humble, but I was actually fixing my thoughts and prayers almost entirely on myself. I was ignoring the complete forgiveness and grace Jesus extended to me, and I was living in my own self-constructed purgatory instead.

But now, I know the key to fighting and overcoming that feeling of shame. We have the power to alter our own reality by letting go of our troubles and insecurities and instead focusing on worshipping God. If we keep our eyes on all that is beautiful and good, we can allow God's goodness to seep into the difficult and painful places in our lives. In Isaiah 6:3, the angels proclaim, "Holy, holy, holy is the LORD Almighty; the whole earth is full of his glory." The world is also full of sin and sadness, but the angels chose to bask in God's glory and see all of creation in light of that glory. I'm not telling you to live in a fantasy world of denial, but so often we choose to overlook the beauty God has crafted around us—the embrace of our sweet children, the warm sun on our faces—and focus our thoughts on burdens and stressors.

Worshipping is like choosing to go outside and enjoy a warm summer day even though you have a messy house to clean. You're not necessarily in denial of the piles of dishes and laundry that await you inside the house, but it's easier to ignore your burdens when you're basking in the sun. Then, when you're ready to go back inside, you'll have renewed energy and motivation to tackle your chores. Worshipping God is our way of transcending this broken, sinful world and focusing on its perfect, loving Creator. Romans 12:12 tells us, "Do not conform to the ways of the world, but be transformed by the renewing of your mind." Renew your mind through worship, and you will be free to live freely in grace.

Sweet friends, God sees you as full of potential and covered in forgiveness and grace. Draw near to Him; focus on the truth of His love, power, and provision. Then You will learn to see yourself the way He sees you and live out the plan He has for you, a life of freedom and purpose.

Questions to Ponder

- How do you choose to view the world? How do you choose to view God? Do you see Him as a mighty, yet loving, Father who works all things for good?

- Are you able to truthfully and joyfully declare that the whole earth is filled with God's glory? If not, are you keeping your eyes on Him and looking for His love and beauty woven throughout creation?

- What burdensome thoughts can you release to live a more abundant life? Give those negative thoughts to God, replace them with scriptural Truth, and thank Him for His continual mercy!

Faith-Filled Ideas

When we worship God for who He is, we re-center our minds on the ultimate Truth. The statements and verses below are foundational to Christianity, but it is easy to forget them when life happens. Write the four verses below (or any others that will encourage you and remind you of the Truth) on sticky notes, and put them in a place where you will see them every day. Each day, read them aloud, and thank God for the encouraging truth in His Word.

Make it a point to teach your kids about at least one of these verses this week. Pray and look for an opportunity to apply God's Word to their lives and in their struggles, so that they will internalize God's message of love.

- God is good even though He allows bad things to happen in the world (Isaiah 55:8-9).

- God is always there, loving us and guiding us even when we feel alone and abandoned (Proverbs 3:5-6).

- God has good plans for those who love and follow Him even when life seems hopeless (Romans 8:28).

- God has good plans for you (Colossians 3:12).

journal

Worship

Journal

Worship

> "I appeal to you, therefore, brothers, by the mercies of God, to present your bodies as a living sacrifice, holy and acceptable to God, which is your spiritual worship.
>
> ~ Romans 12:1 (ESV)

"You can have it all, Lord;
Every part of my world;
Take this life and breathe on this heart that is now Yours."
   ~ Bethel Music

- As you meet with the Lord, thank Him that His mercies are new every day and that He has a plan for your day (Lamentations 3:22-23; Jeremiah 29:11).

- Read Jeremiah 29:11-14. As you read, reflect on the promises in these verses. Journal what these promises mean to you.

- Take a moment to dwell on the goodness of the Lord, His overwhelming love, and who He is.

A Life of Praise

By: Katie Sadler

Sunday morning worship was beautiful and moving. As I lifted my hands to worship my King, my heart was moved to surrender. I love worship services because I know I meet with Jesus there. The Bible tells us that God inhabits the praises of His people, so you can see why a congregation singing His praise is the perfect place to meet with Him.

Coming home to my to-do list, I began to wonder how I could keep this position of worship in my heart throughout the day. Do I turn on a worship album and sing along? When I do, I get lost in the worship and don't accomplish much. That wasn't the answer my heart was looking for, so I asked the Lord.

Two verses came to my mind:

> Present your bodies as a living sacrifice, holy and acceptable to God, which is your spiritual worship. (Romans 12:1 ESV)

> The true worshipers will worship the Father in spirit and truth, for the Father is seeking such people to worship him. (John 4:23 ESV)

I pondered these verses for a few days, trying to understand how to incorporate worship into everyday living. Then, among the laundry, it was clear to me. God wants all that I do to bring Him glory (1 Corinthians 10:31). If God knows the plans He has for me (Jeremiah 29:11) and has given me the life of wife and mother, my spiritual act of worship is to bring His name glory in all I do. Whether I am folding clothes, running to activities, or preparing a meal, I worship by honoring God in the tasks set before me.

Being a living sacrifice is what my dad always calls "dying to yourself." It's putting my grumbling heart aside and refocusing on the Lord and His ways, presenting all I do as a gift. In John 4, Jesus tells the woman at the well that we will worship in spirit and truth.

So what is worship?

Worship

Worship is an act of *devotion* usually directed towards a deity. An act of worship may be performed individually, in an informal or formal group, or by a designated leader.

Did you catch that? Worship is an act of devotion. We know how to show our devotion to our family and friends; that seems easy. It's the same for God. Living our lives with a heart of devotion towards our Creator and Savior spills over into all we do. When we live to show Him our devotion, we live sacrificial lives because we love Him more than we want to do things our way.

Worship is the position of our hearts. It is focusing on who we are worshipping and why we do what we do. Worship is not merely songs of praise, but it is a life of praise.

This season, as you learn how to abide in Jesus, let a heart of worship draw you further into His presence and deeper into the Vine, for there is life when we abide in the Vine.

Questions to Ponder

• When you hear the word "worship," what comes to mind?

• If you don't already, how can you begin to see worship as a heart position, instead of singing songs?

• How can you present yourself as a living sacrifice throughout your day?

Faith-Filled Ideas

Begin your day with some worship music playing. Ask the Lord how to make your to-do list an act of worship. Remember, the music isn't the worship, but having it on will remind your mind that your heart is worshipping in all you do.

Take a minute to write yourself a couple of reminders to live as a worshipper. Hand-letter or paint a reminder, find a graphic online you like and print it off, or simply grab a sticky note and jot it down.

Invite your children to join in as you worship with music. This will be a sweet time to share with them. As you go about your day, remind them about the time you spend with the Lord and incorporate it into what you are doing; for example, tell them, "The way we share our toys is an act of worship. It shows others the love of Jesus." Just little things here and there will help them begin to understand that worship isn't only singing at church.

Worship

journal

_____

_____

_____

_____

_____

_____

_____

_____

journal

_____

Food for the Soul

A sweet and personal time for me is when I worship the Lord. It makes me feel closer to Him, can change my foul mood into a pleasant one, lift my soul, and give peace to my heart and mind. "Sing to the Lord, all the earth: proclaim his salvation day after day" (1 Chronicles 16:23). We listen to Christian music quite a lot in our home, but weekend mornings are special. We go to the late service at church on Sunday mornings so we can have a slower, more relaxed rhythm in our house. On these days, I get up, turn on worship music in the kitchen, and make a big breakfast for my family. When we have an extra bit of time, I will treat them to homemade crepes.

We absolutely love crepes, but feeding all seven of us takes a little bit of time. Crepes are so versatile—they can be either sweet or savory, and can be filled up with just about anything. You can get very creative when making crepes, although my absolute favorite combination is Nutella and strawberries. Don't be too intimidated to try making them! Practice makes perfect, and the more mistakes you make, the more you get to snack on while making them! This recipe is based on Alton Brown's recipe from his *Good Eats, The Early Years* cookbook. He uses a lot of weight measurements, so I have done my best to convert them for easy use.

CREPES By: Brandi Carson

Basic Crepe Ingredients:
2 large eggs

¾ cup whole milk

½ cup water

1 cup flour

4 tablespoons unsalted butter, melted and cooled

Sweet Crepe Variation:
¼ cup white sugar

1 teaspoon vanilla

Savory Crepe Variation:
¼ teaspoon salt

Directions:

1. Place the eggs, milk, water, flour, melted butter, and additional ingredients for either sweet or savory crepes in a blender and blend for 7-10 seconds or until there are no lumps and batter is smooth. Rest batter in refrigerator for 1 hour.

2. Heat a large, lightweight non-stick skillet over medium heat, and coat with butter or cooking spray.

3. Pour ¼ cup of batter into the heated pan. Swirl the pan while pouring the batter, and use an icing spatula to spread it around evenly, creating a nice, even, smooth circle. Pouring the batter will take some practice until you get the hang of the motion. Crepes are very thin and almost stretchy in texture.

4. Cook crepe for 30 seconds or until the edge is lightly browned and turn heat up slightly. Flip and cook for an additional 10 seconds.

5. Set finished crepe aside, cover it with a hand towel, and repeat the process.

These crepes also freeze well. If you have time to make a big batch all at once, you can store some for another day. Just let them cool completely and store in an airtight freezer bag.

Variations: For **sweet crepes**, fill with different fruits or berries, Nutella, peanut butter, or sweet creams. The possibilities are endless! For **savory crepes**, fill with eggs, spinach, cheeses, and lunch or breakfast meats. You are only limited by your imagination!

Worship
~ Week Two ~

Hello Sweet Mamas!

May I share a secret with you? When I'm feeling far away from God, one of the best ways to find Him again is through worship.

By the way, it's not that God has gone anywhere. It's me. I can't sense His presence because I'm too busy. When I'm overwhelmed and anxious about how I will accomplish everything my life demands, I become unable to hear from Him, and I feel alone and empty.

My friend, this is the comforting truth I have found: God's presence never leaves you, and worshipping Him will always fully satisfy your emptiness and allow you to return to and abide in Him.

My loneliness, anxiety, depression, and overwhelmed condition slip away when I sit down at my piano or put my earbuds in and sing to God. My heart is reminded that He who made the heavens, earth, sun, and sky can handle whatever life throws at me. He is bigger than all of it, no matter what it is!

In worship, I surrender to Him. I lay my problems at His feet. I am strengthened and restored.

This week, God wants to hold your hand and guide you to approach His throne with an offering of worship. Whether you're an accomplished musician or can't sing at all, God loves your praise and is blessed by your vulnerable desire to please Him, know Him, and abide in Him more by worshipping Him.

May God bless you and your family this week as you worship God!

Love,
Kristi Valentine and the Help Club for Moms Team

> *Come, let us bow down in worship, let us kneel before the LORD our Maker;*
> *for he is our God and we are the people of his pasture,*
> *the flock under his care.*
>
> *~ Psalm 95:6-7a*

*"I am the vine; you are the branches. If you remain
in me and I in you, you will bear much fruit..."* ~ John 15:5

The Wise Woman Builds Her Spirit

- Pick an attribute of God (Omnipotence, Omniscience, Omnipresence) and do a word study. Find verses that help explain the meanings of the words. Pray for revelation from the Holy Spirit and dive deep.

- Pray Ephesians 3:14-19 over your heart and the hearts of your family members, that you would each be empowered by the Holy Spirit to know how wide, long, high, and deep is the love of God for you.

The Wise Woman Loves Her Husband

- Try something new with your husband, something you both have never done. It doesn't have to be extravagant (eat something different, plan an adventure). Create new memories!

- Clean out your husband's car with your children. Leave a sweet note for him to find that reminds him of your love.

The Wise Woman Loves Her Children

- Play Bible Songs such as "Cedarmont Kids" music or "Wee Sing Bible Songs" in the car instead of watching DVD's. Your kids will hum and sing good, old-fashioned music throughout the day.

- Go into your children's rooms every night this week, gently lay your hand on them, and pray that they would have a heart to know God (Jeremiah 24:7), that they would be the light and salt for Jesus (Matthew 5:13-16), and that they would know and show the love of their Father (1 John 4:19).

The Wise Woman Cares For Her Home

- Utilize the Weekly Plan Sheet and take 20 minutes Sunday afternoon to plan out your week. Strategize and set yourself up for success.

- Try one or all of these fun fall ideas: bake pumpkin bread, hang a pretty fall wreath on your front door, roast pumpkin seeds, or decorate your table or mantle with fun fall decor.

> " Shout for joy to the Lord, all the earth.
> Worship the Lord with gladness; come before him with joyful songs. "
> ~ Psalm 100:1-2

"I'll bring You more than a song
For a song in itself
Is not what You have required

You search much deeper within
Through the way things appear
You're looking into my heart."
  ~ Matt Redman "Heart Of Worship"

- It's time to pray with your prayer partner! Remember, prayer moves mountains!

- Dear precious sister, I encourage you to sit quietly today and listen to praise and worship music during your quiet time. Meditate on the *holiness of* God.

- After a time of reflection, open the Scriptures to read Psalms 29:2, Psalms 95:6, Psalms 109:30, Luke 4:8, and John 4:24. Copy these verses in your journal.

Radical Worship

By: Rae-Ellen Sanders

What exactly is worship? Worship is the place of reverent awe that acknowledges who we are in the light of who God is. When we worship, we reach into the spiritual realm. It's where God communicates with man's spirit or soul through the free gift of the Holy Spirit (John 14:16-17). It is a place where a man cannot hide from the presence of God and where his deepest thoughts are known. God gives us this gift of worship to lift us above the circumstances of earthbound living. The joy we experience is a taste of heaven in our humanity. Have you ever experienced this raw and awesome place in your spirit-self during worship? Worship exceeds tradition and culture and allows us this personal access to the throne room. It is the only eternal activity that transcends time, space, and circumstance. The elders and angels exemplify this as they bow down and praise our Heavenly Father (Revelation. 4:10, Revelation 7:11)!

We were made to worship! God doesn't care if we sing on key; He simply cares that we *sing!* It is not the song that is important to God, but the heart of the worshipper. I like how Jack Hayford describes someone who worships: "Worship changes the worshipper into the image of the One worshipped." Seeking the Lord in sincere worship will transform us and draw us into the presence of Almighty God!

Songs, however, are imperative to worship, and as children of God, we exist to glorify our Creator. Did you know the Bible says that even the rocks will cry out in praise and that the trees will clap their hands?!

> You will go out in joy and be led forth in peace; the mountains and hills will burst into song before you, and all the trees of the field will clap their hands. (Isaiah 55:12)

Praise is driven not by our emotions, but by our will. Matt Redman, recording artist and worship leader, says this about worship, "Revelation of God is the fuel for the fire of worship." When we acknowledge God as almighty and desire Him over everything else, we are essentially fueled to

Worship

worship. Whether it is singing, reverently laying before the Lord, or jumping up and dancing, our circumstances don't have anything against the power of praise!

We are to praise God in *all* situations—in victory and in defeat, when we are in need, and when we have plenty. In fact, the times we don't feel like praising God are actually the very moments that we should. The next time you feel discouraged or defeated, start praising the Lord! When your children are having a meltdown or your marriage is shaky, praise the Lord! God is rich in mercy to those who call upon Him. When you choose to break out into unrestrained worship at the midnight hour of your life, watch out! Heaven may begin to rock the foundations of your life to set you free from the circumstances that bind you.

Start your time in worship by practicing the art of being still—deliberately turn off the noise. Jesus made sure to remove Himself to find strength and to hear from God the Father. Stillness will bring assurance, calm, and peace to your mind and soul.

According to Psalm 100, we are to, "Enter His gates with thanksgiving and His courts with praise," giving thanks to Him and praising His name. To enter into the Holy of Holies (presence of God), we need to first reconcile with the Lord and ask Him to cleanse us. When we knock, He says He will answer (Revelation 3:20). When we ask Him to forgive our sin, He graciously forgives (Acts 13:38-39). We will be free to worship unrestrained, for the blood of Jesus sets us free! God is such a perfect gentleman that He gently holds His nail-pierced hands out for us to surrender our sins to Him. Whatever burdens you may have, lay them down, and then start singing!

Singing pleases the Lord! Every tribe and every heart will sing, and every knee will bow to the risen King! Psalm 98:5 urges us to "make music to the Lord with the harp, with the harp and the sound of singing." And Isaiah 35:10 states, "and those the Lord has rescued will return. They will enter Zion with singing; everlasting joy will crown their heads. Gladness and joy will overtake them, and sorrow and sighing will flee away."

Another way to worship the Lord is by singing verses from the Bible. God's Word contains life and the power to renew our minds, heal our brokenness, and change our lives. It gives us direction for every problem we face. It's God's love letter to us, full of promises to His children. Confessing God's Word saves us from sin and brings us into a personal, intimate relationship with Him. Try singing the words and make up your own tune—may praise be ever on your lips! This is also a fantastic way to learn and teach Scripture because singing helps us remember. Try putting a verse to a tune, and see how soon you and your children are humming and reciting God's Word!

Put your hands up as you worship: This is a form of trust and proclaims your faith. Relieve your yoke by raising your hands to heaven, and the shackles that want to hold you back will be broken in the victory of Jesus' name! Jesus wants to make your yoke easy and your burden light (Matthew 11:30).

Enhance your worship experience by kneeling while you sing and praise the Lord. We need to live day in and day out in this spiritual position of submission to the King of Kings. God says in the Prophets and in the New Testament that every knee will bow before Him (Isaiah 45:23, Romans 14:11, Philippians 2:10). Submission is a state of total helplessness and the mark of a true servant who has no plans of his own. The true servant exists only to fulfill and execute the will of his Master. Face-down worship is a symbol of total surrender.

Questions to Ponder

• What does your worship look like?

• Do you raise your hands in abandoned worship?

• Do you ever sing God's Word out loud?

Worship

• Has the Holy Spirit been prodding you to let go of others' opinions and worship Him as I described above?

Charles Spurgeon says it best:

> I believe that in public worship we should do well to be bound by no human rules, and constrained by no stereotyped order.

Get your song back, and don't let the enemy mute you!

Faith-Filled Ideas

Don't be just a Sunday worshipper!

- Worship at home and make it a daily routine!
- Encourage your family to dance and worship with you. Even your husband will feel his burdens lift as he dances around the living room! If he thinks it's not manly, remind him that King David danced!

journal

_____

_____

_____

_____

_____

_____

_____

_____

_____

_____

_____

_____

_____

_____

_____

_____

Worship

> " For my thoughts are not your thoughts,
> neither are your ways my ways, declares the Lord. "
>
> ~ Isaiah 55:8 (ESV)

"The life of discipleship is not the hero-worship we would pay to a good master, but obedience to the Son of God."
~ Dietrich Bonhoeffer

- Hello moms, Let's talk about worshipping by living out the truth of God's Word as a form of worship.

- "Worship," as defined in the 1828 Webster's Dictionary, means to honor with extravagant love and extreme submission. As you dig into today's study, ponder this definition, and invite God to give you ears to hear what He may whisper into your heart today.

- Opeon up your Bible and read Isaiah 55:8 and Isaiah 30:21. Write both of these powerful verses in your journal.

Wisely Choose His Way

By: Jennifer Kindle

Gathering around our dinner table one evening, my family cracked open the Bible to check how each person's behavior stood up against the truth of God's Word. Tension had been building among our children, emotions were heightened, and hearts were tender.

My husband and I asked our children, "What does submitting to Truth look like? Are we truly loving each other?"

One child clearly announced his knowledge of God's Word to answer the first question, but knowledge alone can't answer the second. We reminded him that what's often harder than knowing God's Word is living by that Word and letting it transform you.

In return, we posed the question, "Has it become you?" Eyes turning up, he listened, and we continued, "Knowledge is just information, but wisdom is applying that information. What you know needs to become who you are."

As we abide in Christ, renewing our minds with truth, letting God align our hearts, and submitting to who He is, we are strengthened to die to our fleshly desires and let His love live through us. Letting God change our hearts into His likeness is a sincere and powerful form of worship. Letting God live and love through us is the catalyst that reveals to those around us the God who is our source of worship.

For us moms, the daily routine of motherhood provides plenty of opportunities to lay down our lives and submit to God's will over our own. Our heart's desire as Christian mothers is to be women who model the character of Christ by walking in obedience to God and choosing to make the most of every opportunity. Just like our children found that discussing what the Bible says about living peacefully is easier than actually doing it, I am often reminded that knowing I should model Jesus to my family is harder than it seems.

In my own struggle to love like Christ, I often fail to respond to the way my Father is calling me to walk by His loving Word. There are days when I impatiently insist on my own way, and others when I'm quick to anger and slow to offer grace. I react to my children's missteps instead of responding with the patience and gentleness that Jesus has demonstrated for us. I try so hard, but parenting is tough! No matter how well we know the Scriptures or the latest parenting techniques, no one can be a perfect parent, and God doesn't expect that from us. But He does want us to make it our daily aim to obey what we read in the Word of God, and to do that by the power of His Holy Spirit. It is not by our might, or by our power, but by His Spirit (Zechariah 4:6).

God will help us choose to obey and abide in Jesus over our fleshly desires and even our to-do lists, and, when we do, we are truly worshipping Him. By exalting God and choosing to worship Him through our daily attitudes and obedience, even when they are not 100% perfect, we are worshipping God. We are living out the good guideline given to us in 1 Corinthians 13:4-7 (ESV) that shows us the godly and loving attitudes we should aspire to live out:

> Love is patient and kind; love does not envy or boast; it is not arrogant or rude. It does not insist on its own way; it is not irritable or resentful; it does not rejoice at wrongdoing, but rejoices with the truth. Love bears all things, believes all things, hopes all things, endures all things.

Has love become who you are? It is a helpful gift for the Lord to instruct us by offering, "This is the way, walk in it." Choose patience, act kindly, be gentle, consider others better than yourself, outdo one another in showing honor, go the extra mile, and serve with a grateful heart. Model this lifestyle for your children, and pray that they will learn to do the same. Wholly submitting to God, who He is, and how He calls us to live is our greatest act of worship.

Questions to Ponder

• Do you recognize that your fleshly desires are not His desires?

• Do you acknowledge that His ways are higher and bring more peace than your ways?

• Ask God for help to obey what He tells you to do in His Word. He will help you. In fact, He doesn't even want you to try to do anything alone (John 15:5). Rejoice in this truth today!

Faith-Filled Ideas

Read 1 Corinthians 13:4-7 again and ask God to highlight the areas that you need to work on in order to grow into His likeness.

Take one truth, one Scripture, one word, and let it become who you are, even if it takes an entire year. It would be better for God to grow you into His likeness over an entire year than for a year to be wasted on more knowledge that isn't applied.

_____

_____

journal

_____

_____

_____

_____

_____

_____

_____

_____

_____

_____

_____

_____

_____

_____

_____

_____

_____

_____

_____

_____

_____

_____

_____

_____

_____

_____

Worship

> Great are YOU, Lord. You are great and greatly to be praised. You are feared above all gods. All the gods of people are idols, but You, Lord, made the heavens. Splendor and majesty are before You. Strength and beauty are in Your sanctuary.
>
> ~ Psalm 96: 4-6

"Worship-based prayer seeks the face of God before the hand of God. God's face is the essence of who He is. God's hand is the blessing of what He does. God's face represents His person and presence. God's hand expresses His provision for needs in our lives. I have learned that if all we ever do is seek God's hand, we may miss His face; but if we seek His face, He will be glad to open His hand and satisfy the deepest desires of our hearts."
~ Daniel Henderson, Transforming Prayer

- It's time to meet with Jesus. Put away all media devices. If you're using a device to read the Bible study, put it on Do Not Disturb and close all the other apps.

- Read Psalm 96. Read it out loud, with intentionality, so you believe every word you say.

Worship-Based Prayer

By: Daphne Close

I love to worship God. I also love to sing. Coincidence? Yes. A big misconception among Christians is that singing is the only way to worship God. Actually, worship encapsulates so much more than words set to music.

So why does the Psalm that we read for today's study first tell us to sing? Singing is a response that comes from our souls' longings to burst out with all that we think and feel about God. This comes from a genuine practice of worship.

Did you know that the history of the word worship comes from "worth-ship"? In other words, God is worthy of everything noble, honorable, valuable, beautiful, and more. When we worship, we do not simply thank God for what He does. We praise Him for who He is!

The key to filling your soul with the presence of God does not begin at church or with other Christians. The Bible mandates public worship, as indicated by its talk about the body of Christ. Donald Whitney writes in *Spiritual Disciplines for the Christian Life*: "Can we expect the flames of our worship of God to burn brightly in public on the Lord's Day when they barely flicker for Him in secret on other days?" In other words, we must discipline ourselves to worship individually!

My church practices a concept called worship-based prayer. It has not only changed the way I pray, but it has also opened my eyes to see more of Him. The more I see Him, the more I want to worship Him.

Compare the following examples of prayer:
- I praise You, for You are good to me.
- God, You are good.

Do you see how the object of the prayer shifts to having God as the center of focus rather than yourself? They are both heartfelt, scripturally-based prayers, but when you compare the two, you will see how important it is to talk about God alone—not about you—simply God.

Some other examples of worship-based prayer derived from Scripture:

- "'Holy, holy, holy is the Lord God Almighty,' who was, and is, and is to come." (Revelation 4:8)

- "Lord, our Lord, how majestic is your name in all the earth!" (Psalm 8:1)

Go ahead and try these examples. Notice that these prayers are sentences, not lengthy paragraphs. Keep your words of worship simple. If you practice worship-based prayer, I believe the Holy Spirit will sanctify you greatly. You will think less of yourself and more of God. Your soul will overflow with a desire to declare God as worthy. You may even unexpectedly and unabashedly burst out in song!

Questions to Ponder

- Remember, dear sister in Christ, God wants you to worship Him at all times, no matter the circumstance. Read these three passages: 2 Samuel 6:14-15; 2 Samuel 12:19-20; Job 1:18-22.

  Ask yourself:

  1. Why does King David/Job worship?

  2. How does he worship?

  3. Will I worship no matter the circumstance?

Faith-Filled Ideas

Sit at the feet of Jesus. Worship Him by completing this statement. God, You are _____. Fill the blank with ten different characteristics of God. Don't fret if you can't think of ten characteristics of God. Remember, worship is a discipline, so it takes practice.

Read Psalm 96:4-6 aloud, but change it into a worship-based prayer: *Great are **You**, Lord. You are great and greatly to be praised. You are feared above all gods. All the gods of people are idols, but You, Lord, made the heavens. Splendor and majesty are before You. Strength and beauty are in Your sanctuary.*

The description in this study for worship based prayer is only the beginning. For a much more in-depth explanation, go to http://www.strategicrenewal.com/worship-based-prayer.

Worship

Journal

_____

_____

_____

_____

_____

_____

_____

journal

_____

_____

_____

_____

_____

_____

_____

_____

_____

_____

_____

_____

_____

_____

_____

_____

_____

_____

_____

_____

_____

_____

_____

_____

_____

_____

_____

Worship

Worship ~ Week Two ~ Day Six

Journal

Worship

Hearing God
~ Week One ~

Sweet Friends,

As we dive into the topic of "Hearing God," there are a few things to note:

- **When we stop to hear from God, we know where to go!**
  If you find yourself in a season where you are unsure of where to go or what to do, Jesus is calling you. He wants you to hear from Him!

- **When we hear from God, He brings healing.**
  The very presence of Jesus in our lives brings healing to our souls, especially when we are certain that He is talking to us and cares for us! His love is a balm like no other!

- **It takes practice!**
  Sometimes it doesn't feel easy to hear from God, but that doesn't mean He isn't talking to us and guiding us. It simply means we are out of practice of going to Him and learning to hear from Him. We can hear God in so many ways: interacting with someone we love, worshipping in song or prayer, reading our Bible, or consulting a friend or mentor. If you are out of practice, mama, you are in the right place!

We pray that you "Hear from God" and that your relationship with Him is closer and sweeter because of it!

With Love,
Krystle Porter and the Help Club for Moms Team

> *Prayer is first of all listening to God. It's openness. God is always speaking; he's always doing something. Prayer is to enter into that activity... Convert your thoughts into prayer. As we are involved in unceasing thinking, so we are called to unceasing prayer. The difference is not that prayer is thinking about other things, but that prayer is thinking in dialogue... a conversation with God.*
>
> *~ Henri Nouwen*

Mom Tips

"I am the vine; you are the branches. If you remain in me and I in you, you will bear much fruit..." ~ John 15:5

The Wise Woman Builds Her Spirit

• Take time this week to listen to God. If you don't always hear Him that's okay, this exercise can help. Pull out your journal, ask God to speak to you. Start writing the questions you've been wrestling with in your mind. Be bold and don't hold back. God desires to hear your thoughts. After a few moments, stop. Listen and write what He speaks to you. It takes practice to be able to discern the Lord's voice, so this is a great start. Reread the journal entry and you'll be amazed how God has answered your questions.

• Write John 10:27 on your mirror with dry erase marker. Work on memorizing it this week.

The Wise Woman Loves Her Husband

• Leave an encouraging note for your husband to find later in his work day, like his lunchbox or bathroom mirror, to let him know you're thinking of him and that you think he is wonderful.

• Put your kids to bed a little early and play a game of cards or a two-player board game (Scrabble, Yahtzee, etc.) with your husband.

The Wise Woman Loves Her Children

• Encourage positive self-talk among your children every day this week. Every time you hear them say "I can't" or "I am not good enough," stop and tell them "they can" and "they are good enough." Have them turn the negative statement into a positive one. Remind them they are children of God who are fearfully and wonderfully made. Encourage them to memorize Psalm 139:14 to help banish negative self-talk.

• Plan a hike and encourage your children to listen for the Lord's voice and feel His presence as they walk. Tell them that hearing from God and feeling His presence can be as simple as looking around at nature and noticing the beauty. Be sure to gather supplies to make homemade trail mix; cheerios, pretzels, nuts, chocolate, etc. Yummy snacks make hiking fun!

The Wise Woman Cares For Her Home

• Make sure to have the dishes in the dishwasher, floor swept, and counters wiped down each night before you go to bed.

• If you plan to hand out candy to trick or treaters, turn it into a fun ministry project. Before the evening begins, pray for every person who will come to your door. Ask Jesus to show them His love and for them to come to know Him as their Savior if they don't already. You can also make cards that say "Jesus Loves You" with John 3:16 printed on them. Hand these cards out with your candy.

> **"** The eyes of the LORD are on the righteous,
> and his ears are attentive to their cry. **"**
>
> ~ Psalm 34:15

"The facts are that God is not silent, has never been silent. It is the nature of God to speak."
  ~ A.W. Tozer, *The Pursuit of God*

- Have you made your weekly prayer call? Habitually discussing God and praying with a friend is a great way not only to hear His voice, but also to confirm that it is His voice you're hearing.

- Grab your Bible, a journal, and refreshing beverage. Find a quiet place to relax, remove all distractions, and focus on God's Word.

- Write Psalm 34:15 in your journal. Remember that our righteousness comes through Jesus' sacrifice and God's mercy, not our own ability to avoid sin; therefore, this promise applies to you!

Hearing God Over the Background Noise

By: Heather Doolittle

Friends, the past couple of years have been hard for my family and me. We have experienced more difficult situations in such a short time than I would have thought possible, and it has led me to a realization; we are lambs among wolves. We have no human defense against the powers of Hell that attack us, and so we must rely fully on God. But how does that look when hard times come, emotions cloud our judgment, and none of our options seem sufficient? How do we discern the voice of the Holy Spirit from the background noise of culture and selfishness? The answer is fervent, passionate, faithful prayer and fasting.

The Bible instructs us to pray about everything, not just the obviously important decisions (Philippians 4:6). You never know when God has big plans for something that appears insignificant. Your Father wants to do life with you every day; He wants to be your confidant, the first One you turn to with exciting news as well as complicated problems. Isn't it comforting to picture your Heavenly Father – the embodiment of Love and Grace—with you constantly, guiding you in every decision? He is here, but you need to lean into Him to experience His presence and provision. Quiet your mind and listen to the still, small voice inside your heart (1 Kings 19:12). You have the Power of God in you; own it and live it out (Romans 8:11)! Don't live like those who have a measure of godliness, but deny its power (2 Timothy 3:5).

Sometimes we are too close to a situation to set aside our emotions and desires long enough to hear God; and in this case, it's helpful to have the opinions of trusted, godly advisors. Matthew 18:20 confirms this truth: "For where two or three gather in my name, there am I with them." What a

Hearing God

wonderful picture—gathering in prayer around God! Seek out godly women who are further ahead of you in life, in spiritual maturity, or in parenting stages. Consulting with friends and mentors provides a valuable outside perspective and often confirms what God is speaking to you, but be careful not to gossip or vent. Keep the discussion positive, focusing on timeless scriptural truths instead of conventional, worldly wisdom.

Then there are times when the world is so convincing, and our desires so strong, that the right path is not very clear, even after fervent prayer. That is when fasting is most useful. Combining prayer with fasting helps to eliminate the background noise from our lives so we can shift our focus to God. It is not a special formula to see into God's crystal ball, but rather a way to clear our minds and open our hearts to His voice.

I used to avoid fasting because blood sugar issues prevented it, but I've since learned that there are many ways to fast. The heart of fasting is about abstaining from distractions, not necessarily food. In Old Testament days, feeding your family was a much bigger deal than it is now. You would have had to harvest/slaughter your meal, cook it from scratch without a microwave or slow cooker, and hand wash all the dishes. One benefit to cutting out eating was that it added hours to the day! What can you remove from your routine to provide extra time with God? Try turning off your TV for the week or going a day without answering calls, texts, emails, and social media. Then give that extra time to God; don't squander it.

God blessed Jacob for struggling with the angel (Genesis 32:22-32) because He knows that those who struggle—those who go to the extra effort to seek out God, His blessings, and His guidance—will find Him. Prayer is a means of inserting God into every aspect of our thoughts and lives; fasting is a practical method of deepening that prayer relationship with God. He is capable of so much more than you could ever ask or imagine, so don't give up—keep searching and have faith (Ephesians 3:20)!

Questions to Ponder

- Do you pray about everything? Be honest with yourself. Ask God how you can live your life more prayerfully in sync with Him.

- What can you fast that would provide extra time and turn your focus toward God?

Faith-Filled Ideas

Plan a day or two to fast in the next couple of weeks, and determine in advance the conditions of your fast. This will help you to be firm since you'll be tempted to compromise when the time comes. Thoughts like "checking emails doesn't really count as media" and "drinking a little juice isn't actually eating" will come to mind during the fast. Make sure you plan ahead to set aside extra time for prayer during your fast to make the most of it.

Fasting provides an excellent opportunity to share your faith with your children since it is a physical expression of your prayer life. Explain to them what you're doing and ask them to help you stick to it (they can help make their own lunches if you're fasting food or keep the TV off if you're fasting media). Maybe they'll want to join you by giving up screen time or sweets for a day, but don't pressure them into it. You can't force anyone (not even your own children) to draw near to God. They can learn by observing you.

Hearing God

journal

_____

_____

_____

_____

_____

_____

_____

_____

_____

_____

_____

_____

_____

_____

_____

_____

_____

_____

_____

_____

_____

_____

_____

_____

_____

_____

_____

_____

Hearing God

He tends his flock like a shepherd: He gathers the lambs in his arms and carries them close to his heart; he gently leads those that have young.

~ Isaiah 40:11

"You can only learn so much from books. You can only learn so much from education. Ultimately, it is the wisdom of God that will carry you through in the toughest situations of life."
~ Ravi Zacharias

- It's time to meet with your Jesus. He is the One who longs to hold you close and teach you all you need to know. Rejoice today, knowing that He delights in you, His dear daughter, coming to Him about anything and everything. He loves to hear your voice and He never tires of hearing it.

- Read John 10:27-30. Read the whole chapter if you have time. Write verse 27 in your journal.

Help! I Don't Know What To Do!

By: Deb Weakly

Do you ever get confused with all of the "parenting wisdom" available in the world: to spank or not to spank, timeouts or time-ins, boundaries or no boundaries, homeschool or public school, immunizations or no immunizations? And the list goes on and on and on. It seems like everywhere we turn, we hear conflicting stories about how we should parent our children.

We all want to do our best and raise up successful men and women who love God, so what's a poor mother to do?

I remember feeling so confused as a mom. Not only did I feel inadequate because I wasn't raised in a Christian home and had no idea how to have one, but I also felt lost because of all of the parenting advice out there.

To complicate matters, I had some great friends in my life, but their children weren't the same as mine; theirs were easy and compliant. Their advice wasn't always helpful because they didn't understand everything that was going on. And, to make matters worse, I compared my children's behavior to theirs and felt even more defeated. Then, it would all go downhill from there...

Do you ever feel like I did—overwhelmed and confused about what to do with all of the parenting advice? It doesn't have to be like this. There is another way, and it's really simple; learn to go to God first. He knows your children better than you do. After all, He created them! And He loves your children with a wide and long and high and deep love that exceeds our human understanding.

As a Christ-follower, you have the capability to hear God's voice. You have the Holy Spirit living inside of you and He speaks to you, deep on the inside, especially as you are reading the Bible and whenever you are praying.

I know this may sound oversimplified, but this one habit can change your life and the way you parent your children. It can increase your confidence and help you to feel like a strong mom who knows her kids and how to raise them in the power of the Holy Spirit.

As we learn to listen to God's voice, we can hear Him speaking to us about our children and everything else going on in our lives.

So mama, before you pick up the phone to call a friend or surf the internet for expert advice, simply stop, pick up your Bible, and pray. Advice from other moms and authors is so important, and can really help us to become a good mom (Proverbs 13:20), but the first and foremost place we should go for help is God, then to our husband. But that's another devotion for another day...

Questions to Ponder
- If you were being completely honest, do you go to God first or do you go to people? What would help you to turn to God first?
- Where do you need help? Write it down? Ask God for wisdom in this area.

Faith-Filled Ideas
Establishing a daily quiet time has completely changed my life. You will be amazed at how easy it is and how much it helps.

Here are a few simple ideas I have learned over the years:
- If you do not read the Bible regularly, ask God to help you! Ask Him to give you the time and energy and desire to do it. He wants to help you (John 15:5-8).
- Read your Bible and pray most days, even if it's just for a few moments. As you begin your time with God, ask Him to speak to you. He will! Be sure to pray for wisdom. God will give it to you (James 1:5).
- Make sure to write down anything that you sense God is telling you. It could simply be a Scripture that stood out to you or a specific inclination you may feel in your heart or mind. Write it down and remember to come back to it later on in the week to add anything you may have learned from your other times with God. Regularly look back over your journal to prayerfully identify any patterns in what you are writing down. This just may be your answer (John 16:13).
- If you don't feel like you hear God speak to you, that's okay! The more time you spend praying and reading the Word of God, the easier it will be for you to learn to hear His voice. Understanding the Scriptures and hearing the voice of God is a little like learning a foreign language; the more you practice and speak it, the better you get at it (Romans 12:2).
- Pray with your husband and ask his advice about what's going on with your child or what you are struggling with (Ephesians 5:22-24).
- Pray with a friend. Don't forget that a big component of the Help Club for Moms is praying with a prayer partner! It's soooo powerful to pray regularly with a friend (James 5:16).
- Last, but certainly not least, is to *obey!* Do what God tells you to do in His Word. Ask Jesus to help you to do what He is telling you to do. And remember, God will never tell you to do anything that does not align with the Word of God (2 Timothy 3:16-17).

You can do it, mama! You were made for this! Remember, you are not alone—never, ever, ever. Jesus is with you each and every day.

Hearing God

journal

_____

_____

_____

_____

_____

_____

_____

_____

_____

_____

_____

_____

_____

_____

_____

_____

_____

_____

_____

_____

_____

_____

_____

_____

_____

_____

Hearing God

The voice of the Lord is powerful; the voice of the Lord is full of majesty.
~ Psalm 29:4 (KJV)

"God's voice is still and quiet and easily buried under an avalanche of clamor."
~ Charles Stanley

- It's time to seek the Lord's face! When we bury our faces in God's Word, we reflect His glory! I have seen this reflection on men and women who spend quality time with Jesus. I want this same glow! Read Psalm 105:2-4 and Psalm 63:1-2, write these verses in your journal, and then take a few minutes to read and meditate on the rest of Psalm 63. If you want to go deeper, add Psalm 73:23-28 to your reading today.

Hearing From God

By: Rae-Ellen Sanders

Our purpose as God's creation is to commune with God, to hear His voice, and to follow what He says. Think back to Adam and Eve: their primary purpose in the garden was to walk with the Lord and fellowship with Him. God created them to commune with Him and to be His friends. God wants to talk to us too!

An important step in hearing from God is blocking out distraction. We need to be like the baseball pitcher in the movie, *For Love of the Game*, who blocks out the noisy fans and calms his anxieties to become single-mindedly focused on delivering a pitch. In the film *The Legend of Bagger Vance*, a pro golfer uses this same technique to block out the noise of the crowd and align his swing for success. Like these athletes, we benefit from narrowing our focus and attention on God. When we ignore or put our concerns on hold, we are more apt to hear God's still voice.

If you have trouble hearing from God, carve time out for solitude. We need a sanctuary—a place to meet with God. Begin by asking the Lord's forgiveness for any sin in your life. Come before the Lord in humility. This will put you in right standing with the Holy of Holies!

I once heard a story called "A Gallon of Milk" by an unknown author. In this story, there was a man at a midweek Bible study. The topic was hearing from God, but this man had little experience of hearing God's voice. Wanting to experience this himself, the man asked God to speak to him on the way home. While driving, the Holy Spirit spoke in his ear to stop at the store and buy a gallon of milk. Not sure if the idea was from God or not, he kept driving home. Again he felt he should stop and buy the milk. He remembered the Bible story of how Samuel had heard from the Lord and ran to Eli, so he said: "Is that you, God?" He stopped, obeyed, and bought the milk. As he continued to drive home, he heard in his mind he should drive down a certain street. He passed it up but at once felt like he was to turn around. He wondered if he was imagining the directions. Suddenly, he felt the need to stop in front of a small, dark house. He asked God, "Lord what am I to do? It doesn't look like anyone is home. What if I am wrong?" God prompted him to go to the door and give the milk to whoever came to the door. He lamented that he thought it was insane to just walk up and offer milk to strangers, but he said: "God, if this is you, then I will obey even if it makes me look like a crazy person." So as the story goes, he obediently walked up and rang the doorbell. A man opened the door, and he thrust the jug of milk at him and said: "Here, I bought you some milk." The man just looked at him with a crazy expression and then turned and rushed down the hall. The man returned, carrying a crying baby, and with tears streaming down his face, he explained that they had run out of money and couldn't buy their baby milk. They had just been praying and asking God to provide the milk that they needed. The young man offered what money he could, and as he walked back to his car with tears in his own eyes, he knew that God *does still speak* and *answer prayers*.

I love this story and how it emphasizes that God speaks to His children. Hearing is one thing, but heeding is another. They go hand-in-hand to execute God's plan. Challenge yourself to hear from God and do what He says!

Questions to Ponder

• Do you hear God's still, small voice? Do you reserve time to be still?

• The same Holy Spirit that lives inside of you also lives inside of your children. If they have received Jesus as their Lord and Savior, your kids can hear from God too! Encourage your little ones to be quiet before the Lord and to ask God to give them ears to hear!

Faith-Filled Ideas

I took a spiritual gifts class in college where we were encouraged to ask the Holy Spirit to talk to us through handwriting. We sat with paper and pen, asking the Spirit to download what He wanted to say. Then we just started writing. It was awesome to allow the Holy Spirit to speak through our own hands! Go ahead and try this exercise. God *wants* to talk to us and tell us how much we are loved and valued. He has great plans for us. And He wants us to tell the world about His love, power, and redemptive plan!

If you are confident that you hear from God, do you write down what He says? He speaks through His Word, through His people, and in His still, small voice. Seek the Lord and ask Him to speak to you!

Journal

journal

_____
_____
_____
_____
_____
_____
_____
_____
_____
_____
_____
_____
_____
_____
_____
_____
_____
_____
_____
_____
_____
_____
_____
_____
_____
_____
_____
_____

Hearing God

As a homeschooling mama of five, life can be hectic and busy. I must be very intentional about spending time with God and His Word in order to hear from Him. When our schedule gets too overwhelming, I must simplify life as much as possible to make this happen. And to make dinner easier, I pull out my trusty slow cooker.

Proverbs 31:27 (ESV) reads, "She looks well to the ways of her household and does not eat the bread of idleness." In busy seasons of life, let me tell you, there is no time for idleness. Looking well to the ways of my household sometimes means working smarter, not harder. My slow cooker helps me to feed my family without spending all day in the kitchen. This two-for-one recipe is a simple, set-it-and-forget-it crowd pleaser.

Two Slow Cooker Meals in One:

SHREDDED CHICKEN TACOS & LAYERED TACO CASSEROLE
Plus, a Bonus Recipe for Homemade Taco Seasoning!

By: Brandi Carson

Ingredients:

2-4 pounds chicken breasts

⅓ cup homemade taco seasoning (see recipe below) or one package of store-bought taco seasoning

1 can of chopped green chiles

Directions:

1. Add all ingredients to your crockpot and cook on low for 6-8 hours or high 3-4 hours.

2. Shred chicken with two forks and mix it in with all the yummy juices. Serve the chicken on tortillas, and add your favorite taco toppings. Serve with your favorite Mexican side dishes such as rice and beans.

Note: This makes a lot of chicken! You will use your leftovers for the second recipe. Use them right away or freeze the leftovers and use them the next time you need a quick and easy meal.

MEAL TWO: LAYERED TACO CASSEROLE

Ingredients:

Approximately 2 cups of shredded taco chicken

2 cans of kidney beans, drained or 2-3 cups homemade cooked beans

8 ounces shredded Mexican blend, or your favorite cheese

16-ounce jar of your favorite salsa

20 count package of corn tortilla chips

Note: If you want to sneak in a bit of the green stuff, microwave
a couple cups of frozen spinach or kale and drain and mix it
in with the shredded chicken. I frequently sneak veggies into
meals that wouldn't have them otherwise, like Mexican food, to
add a little more nutritional value for our family.

Directions:

1. Spray your slow cooker with nonstick cooking spray to prevent sticking.

2. Spread a couple of spoonfuls of salsa on the bottom of the slow cooker.

3. Layer three corn tortillas on top of the salsa. (Hint: place two tortillas on each end, tear the third tortilla in half, and fill in the empty gaps to complete the layer).

4. Spread a couple of spoonfuls of salsa evenly over the tortilla.

5. Next, spread a couple of spoonfuls of beans evenly on top of the tortillas. Repeat with chicken, then sprinkle a small handful of cheese on top.

6. Repeat layers until all the beans and chicken are used up.

7. On the top, add a final layer of tortilla with just salsa and cheese on top.

8. Cook on low in your slow cooker for 2-4 hours and top with your favorite toppings: salsa, sour cream, green onion, etc.

If you want to get creative, you can also add corn, pepper, and/or jalapeños to the layers or switch to black beans for more of a Tex-Mex feel.

HOMEMADE TACO SEASONING

Note: Measurements in parenthesis are a quadruple batch quantity. I use taco seasoning often, so I like to have a big batch on hand.

Ingredients:

(1 cup) ¼ cup chili powder

(2 tbsp) 1 ½ teaspoons garlic powder

(2 tbsp) 1 ½ teaspoons onion powder

(4 tsp) 1 teaspoon crushed red pepper flakes
(I usually add less because this can make it a
little spicy for the kids, so keep that in mind)

(2 tbsp) 1 ½ teaspoons dried oregano

(2 tbsp) 1 ½ teaspoons paprika

(4 tbsp) 1 tablespoon cumin

(4 tbsp) 1 tablespoon Kosher salt

(4 tsp) 1 teaspoon black pepper

Directions:

1. Mix all ingredients together until completely incorporated.

2. Store in a mason jar or airtight container.

Journal

Hearing God
~ Week Two ~

Dear Sister,

As Christians, we want to hear from God. We want to know His plan for us. We want answers to our questions. Wouldn't it be nice to hear the audible voice of God? I have good news! When we believe in Christ as our Savior, He gives us His Holy Spirit to indwell us and teach us all things. Jesus says in John 14:26, "But the Advocate, the Holy Spirit, whom the Father will send in my name, will teach you all things and will remind you of everything I have said to you." When you read God's Word, invite the Holy Spirit to speak to you.

God so graciously gave us His Word in the form of the Bible, faithfully handing it down from generation to generation and providing for its translation into over a thousand languages. As you meditate on the Word of God and memorize it, you allow the Holy Spirit to remind you of what the Bible says at the moment you need it most! The Word of God is alive and active (Hebrews 4:12). It "is God-breathed and is useful for teaching, rebuking, correcting and training in righteousness," (2 Timothy 3:16). It is our guide for living this Christian life!

We pray that the studies you read this week about Hearing God will strengthen your faith as you abide in Christ!

With Love,
Jennifer Valdois and the Help Club for Moms Team

So how do we hear the voice of God? The first thing to do is open your Bible. When you open your Bible, God opens His mouth. The surest way to get a word from the Lord is by getting into God's Word.

~ Mark Batterson

Mom Tips

"I am the vine; you are the branches. If you remain in me and I in you, you will bear much fruit..." ~ John 15:5

The Wise Woman Builds Her Spirit

- When you pray, have a journal ready to not only write down your prayer requests and praises, but also leave space to write what the Lord is telling you. If you've never done this, simply pray and ask the Lord to speak to you, then write what the Holy Spirit tells you. You might be surprised what God wants to speak to your heart.

- Write Ephesians 2:10 on a sticky note and put it on your bathroom mirror. Memorize it and speak it over yourself every time you think negative though

The Wise Woman Loves Her Husband

- Encourage your husband by telling him how proud you are to have married a godly man (especially if he is a new believer). Thank him that He hears from God and wants the best for you and the children.

- Pray for your husband every day this week! Do not pray for how you want God to change him or complain to God about him. Simply pray that God would bless him and that he would know how wide, long, high, and deep is the love of Christ (Ephesians 3:18).

The Wise Woman Loves Her Children

- Take time to pray with your children. Pray for them throughout the day; pray for them at night. Remember, your prayers are timeless. God uses our prayers for our children all of their lives!

- Don't be afraid of your children getting messy. Whether it is dirt, mud, paint, shaving cream, flour, etc. They learn a lot during those types of activities! Washable art supplies are the best!

The Wise Woman Cares For Her Home

- Take back your master bedroom this week. Create a space of calm and relaxation for you and your husband. Clear any piles of clutter, and put away that laundry that seems to pile up in the master bedroom. Spend an extra moment dusting and cleaning the window covering.

- Turn on worship music each day this week, and allow the Holy Spirit to fill your home with joy. "...In [God's] presence there is fullness of joy!" (Psalm 16:11b ESV).

My sheep listen to my voice; I know them, and they follow me.

~ John 10:27

"Learning to clearly distinguish God's voice is invaluable. Instead of going through life blindly, we can have the wisdom of God guide and protect us."
~ Andrew Wommack

- Hello, dear sister! Call your prayer partner for your 10-minute prayer call! God is the one who has the power to work in your heart and the hearts of those you love. Prayer changes everything!

- Today's devotional relays how we can hear God's voice, even though we are ordinary moms. Find a quiet spot in your home and prepare your heart to listen to the voice of your Shepherd. If you are His child, He lives in you!

- Read John 10:1-14.

Hearing the Voice of Our Shepherd

By: Mari Jo Mast

I cannot think of anything more transforming in a person's life than consistently hearing the voice of Jesus. It is one of the greatest benefits of being God's child! Without this ability, we feel lost and left to ourselves. However, just one word from Him can transform the worst of situations.

Here's good news: we can hear God's voice; yes, even us ordinary moms! We were, in fact, created to have intimacy with Him in this way. His voice breaks bondages in our children, reveals insight into our marriage, and delivers peace into relationships in our home. He knows exactly what we need in order to turn any dire situation around, no matter what has gone wrong!

As you read in John 10 today, Jesus said in verses 4b and 5 (NLT), "he walks ahead of them, and they follow him because they know his voice. They won't follow the voice of a stranger; they will run from him because they don't know his voice."

Jesus was trying to explain to the Pharisees that He is the "One" they were looking for, the Messiah. They clearly were not His children because they were not able to receive what He said about Himself. They didn't believe He was who He claimed to be (the Son of God), thus they could not hear Him. My friend, Jesus is the only way to the Father.

Precious Mom, because of Jesus and His Holy Spirit living inside us, we can now hear God speak.

God loves you so much and He deeply desires to have a living and vital relationship with you! This is why He sent Jesus to die for your sin, but He didn't stay in the grave! God rose Him up again and sent His Spirit to live on the inside of you, to fill you with Himself, bringing your spirit to life. If you believe and agree in your heart that Jesus is Lord, that God raised Him from the dead, and you confess this with your mouth, then you are saved (Romans 10:9)! If you are saved, then you are God's child, and if you are God's child, you absolutely have the ability to hear His voice!

However, we often become so busy with the "stuff" in our lives that we forget what David wrote, "Be still and know that I am God" (Psalm 46:10a). It is in stillness that we hear God, not busyness. In 1 Kings 19:12, Elijah heard the Lord's voice in a gentle whisper. Often our hurried lives drown out His "still, small" voice. We must guard against busy, fussy living, which interferes with the quietness in which He speaks.

There are multiple ways in which God speaks. Sometimes we can mistake the Lord's voice for our own thoughts. I love that He can invade us with ideas! Remember to always filter what you think through God's Word because it helps you to know if it's Him relaying a message, because we also have an enemy who tells us things that are not true. By knowing the Word and asking God to help us understand it we can know the difference between true thoughts and untrue thoughts. After all, Jesus is the Word (John 1:1), so we know His voice in our thoughts will always agree with Scripture!

Another way He may communicate is through impressions. Every one of us has, at times, done something we felt was wrong, even as we were doing it, yet we followed our feelings or gave in to pressure from others instead. We had the impression it was wrong, but we went our own way and missed His leading. Learn to pray and ask the Lord for His truth to be revealed. Be sensitive to hear, so you can avoid this pitfall.

"Delight yourself in the Lord; and He will give you the desires of your heart" (Psalm 37:4 NASB). According to the Word, if you delight yourself in the Lord, your heart can be trusted. God will lead you by your desires when your heart is focused on Him.

Of course, God always speaks through Scripture. His written Word is Truth!

A lot of people are asking God to speak when in reality their ears are not hearing. Jesus said, "He who has ears to hear, let Him hear." Learn to be still, listen to understand with your heart, and then obey. He is always wanting to communicate with His children—always. If you are having difficulty hearing, remember the last thing God told you and then do it. God doesn't want us to bypass His voice with disobedience, because He knows what's best for us! He speaks what He speaks for a reason. He knows our beginning and end, and we must learn to trust and obey.

Hearing God will completely transform everything in our life, bringing freedom and peace, which is what we desire. He leads us in paths of righteousness, bringing honor to His name in the process.

Questions to Ponder

- God speaks to His children in multiple ways, including:
  1. Through Scripture
  2. Through prayer
  3. Through the church (the body of believers)
  4. Through our circumstances
  5. Through our desires (if we're delighting in Him)
  6. By impressions
  7. Through our thoughts (filtered through God's Word)
  8. In the stillness or quiet
- Do you believe that God is always speaking? Might there be something preventing you from hearing? Are you taking the effort and time to listen? What can you change about your lifestyle to hear His voice more clearly?

Faith-Filled Ideas

Ask the Holy Spirit to fill you to overflowing today. Spend a few minutes right now being quiet. Acknowledge He lives in you. Pray and ask Him to reveal Himself to you as you wait. Try to hear and understand what He's speaking in your spirit. Ask Him to bring meaning to what you feel He is saying. Write it down. Practice this routine every day.

When you grocery shop, go to the park, or do everyday duties, remember God's Spirit dwells in you and is speaking. Be ever sensitive to His influence in your life by staying aware of this awesome truth.

God is very much alive, and desires to share His deepest feelings and desires with you. You are His child and have a unique purpose—ask Him to reveal it. He will, in time!

journal

_____

_____

_____

_____

_____

_____

_____

_____

_____

_____

_____

_____

_____

_____

_____

_____

> **"** You will seek me and find me when you seek me with all your heart. **"**
> ~ Jeremiah 29:13 (ESV)

"A word from Jesus changed everything."
~ Henry T. Blackaby

- The most important part of your day is upon you. Make it count! Grab your Bible, a journal, a pen, and a mug of something yummy. Come with an expectant heart. The Lord has something to teach us every day; we need only to sit at His feet and listen.

- Read Jeremiah 29:11-13 and journal what God is saying to you.

You Can Hear the Voice of God!

By: Kristi Valentine

The God who formed the sun, the moon, and the stars wants to talk with you—let this incredible truth soak into your heart. His Word confirms it! Today, let's set our minds on two things: we believe that we can hear from God, and we know how to recognize His voice because we abide in Him. When we are confident in hearing from God, we can live the abundant, productive life of joy God designed us to live.

God's Word says we can hear Him speak! John 10:27a (NASB) says, "My sheep hear My voice." Jesus lived in this world with us for three decades and knew us well when He compared us to sheep, declaring that we indeed can hear His voice. Sheep are vulnerable and in need of loving leadership to guide them to places of nourishment and safety. Because of this, they are experts in listening for their shepherd, so they can receive the guidance they innately know they need. Jesus called us sheep because He designed us to abide in, depend on, and discern the call of our Good Shepherd.

Next, we learn that we're capable of discerning God's voice in Isaiah 30:21a (ESV). "And your ears shall hear a word behind you, saying, 'This is the way, walk in it.'" This verse demonstrates the confidence we have because we will hear which decisions and directions God wants us to choose.

Finally, John 16:13 (CEV) tells us, "The Spirit shows what is true and will come and guide you...He will let you know what is going to happen." Jesus was comforting the disciples by telling them they would hear from Him through the Holy Spirit after He ascended to heaven. We can be comforted in the same way! This passage promises us that the Holy Spirit lives within us and will guide us, show us the truth, and tell us what is going to happen.

Honestly though, how do we know it's truly God speaking to us? Thankfully, the Bible answers this question. First of all, it says, "You will seek me and find me, when you seek me with all your heart," Jeremiah 29:13 (ESV). He is looking for us to long for Him with everything in us, nothing less. Second, there are numerous verses in the Bible that direct us to ask, ask, ask God for what we need.

Hearing God

In Jeremiah 33:3, God says He will tell us things that we don't know when we ask Him. Matthew 7:7a,8a says, "Ask, and it will be given to you...For everyone who asks receives." So if our hearts are wholly submitted to seeking God, and we are asking Him for our needs, then the Bible says we can be assured that He will answer.

Once our hearts and our actions are right in God's sight, our last responsibility in hearing from God is to abide in Him and listen. Remember, John 10:27 says that we will know His voice! John 8:47 (NLT) reminds us to gladly listen to the words of God. Hebrews 2:1 admonishes us to "pay the most careful attention" to hearing and obeying God. And finally, 1 Kings 19:12 (ESV) says a "low whisper" describes the voice of God. Our loving Heavenly Father longs to dialog with us, His beloved children. Will you take the time to walk with Him daily and listen?

Questions to Ponder

• If you're like me, you earnestly long to hear from God. After all, He knows the good plans He has for you: "...to prosper you, not to harm you, plans to give you a hope and a future" (Jeremiah 29:11). We want His perfect, abundant will for our lives! How will you know His will unless you hear from Him? Write in your journal how you will carve out more time to listen to Him by reading His Word. Next, write in your journal how you will create more quiet space in your life to follow the Bible's steps for hearing God: seeking Him with your whole heart, asking Him for your needs, and then finally listening for His low whisper.

Faith-Filled Ideas

One of the unique ways I've learned to hear God is to listen attentively for His voice during times of worship. While I'm singing His praises, He has often reminded me of very significant things. One time, a friend was having difficulties and desperately needed an encouraging word. I did not know of her situation, but God prompted me, while I was worshipping, to call her. I was so glad I did! Another time, He gently awakened me to several of my child's unspoken needs. Again, I was completely unaware of this situation until God spoke to my heart during worship. I was able to help and love my child more fully because of God's tender promptings. Next time you are worshipping, keep a pen and a small notepad nearby. If you sense God moving in your heart about something, write it down. Then, worship with your obedience.

journal

_____

_____

_____

_____

_____

_____

_____

_____

journal

_____

_____

_____

_____

_____

_____

_____

_____

_____

_____

_____

_____

_____

_____

_____

_____

_____

_____

_____

_____

_____

_____

_____

_____

_____

Hearing God

> **Trust in the LORD with all your heart; and lean not unto your own understanding. In all your ways acknowledge him, and He shall direct your paths.**
> ~ Proverbs 3:5-6 (NKJV)

"As you read, pause frequently to meditate on the meaning of what you are reading. Absorb the Word into your system by dwelling on it, pondering it, going over it again and again in your mind, considering it from many different angles, until it becomes part of you."
~ Nancy Wolgemuth DeMoss

- It's time to meet with Jesus! Search your heart to see if anything is hindering you from hearing His voice. Confess it now; lay everything at the feet of Jesus. Choose to submit to Him and believe that He will fill you with unspeakable joy and peace.

- Read Psalm 119:169-172 (NASB). If you can, read all the way to verse 176. Say out loud, several times, the second half of verse 169: "Give me understanding according to Your Word."

The Answer Is in His Word

By: Daphne Close

A few years ago, I was seeking the Lord's direction. Based on an innocent comment by my daughter, I was challenged to consider making drastic changes to her current schooling situation. I could have ignored her statement, as she was by no means asking me for a change; it was just a comment about something she didn't like. Though it was an innocent comment, something in me didn't want to let it pass. I told my husband, "Let's pray about it for one week." I even mentioned it to a friend and at the end of the conversation, I said, "I'm sure we won't change anything."

Then I read Mark 16:3. If you've been a Christian for even a few years, you have probably read and heard the resurrection story many times. Because God's Word is the Living Word, even the most familiar of verses can speak to you as if it's brand new. On this particular occasion, this verse stood out to me: "And they asked each other, 'Who will roll the stone away from the entrance of the tomb?'" (Mark 16:3).

Remember, when you read the Bible, it's best to first look at the intended meaning for the original audience before seeing how it applies to you. Mary Magdalene, Mary the mother of James, and Salome went to anoint Jesus' body, but his body was in a tomb that was blocked by a heavy stone. Many imagine the stone as a giant boulder, but even if it was only a couple feet in diameter, it would have been too heavy for the women to move. Nevertheless, they brought the spices. They had no assurance that someone would move the stone for them, yet to their surprise, the stone was rolled away. Moreover, no mere human moved it, an angel rolled the stone away (Matthew 28:2).

I saw the faith of these women despite their impossible task. At this point, I knew without a doubt that the schooling choice I made, if I trusted God, was possible. Jesus would make a way.

Practically speaking, how can we discern the will of God?

1. Read God's Word. This is one Christian discipline where you don't talk; you listen. If you don't see an answer, keep reading. Come back the next day and the day after that. Wait. His answer will come. "I waited patiently for the LORD; he turned to me and heard my cry" (Psalm 40:1). Do not look for a verse only with the intention of how it will apply to your situation. Simply read, look at the original meaning, then ask how it can bring you closer to Jesus. In the Lord's timing, His Word will extend to your situation.

2. Put your trust in the Lord through prayer. Continually ask, *"Lord, I want to see Your will, so I will keep praying and keep committing my Bible reading to You."*

3. Don't trust feelings or logic. I know this is difficult to do, no matter what your personality. The statement "I just have a peace about it" is great. I don't want to knock that sentiment, but please don't use this as your only determining factor. "I've looked at all the pros and cons" works too, but you can easily miss the spiritual component that does not fit into a list. Even when your feelings and logic match, strive to read God's Word until you receive a final confirmation.

4. It's okay to seek godly wisdom from others, but remember, we are all human, so someone else's advice should not replace hearing from the Lord. I cannot emphasize enough to follow #1 and #2 first.

5. Do not look for a verse to support your decision. You may be in danger of reading without learning the original meaning or worse, twisting the Bible to cater to your needs. Read it openly, not focused on the answer, but waiting to see how God will answer. He may surprise you!

Thank God that we have the Holy Spirit because He will always agree with Scripture. If we don't know the Scripture, then we can't *confirm* if what we hear is truly from the Holy Spirit. So, keep reading, my sister in Christ. You can trust that Jesus will reveal His will and when He does, it will be glorious!

Questions to Ponder

• Are you struggling to hear God's will? Will you commit to practicing #1 and #2 on a daily basis?

Faith-Filled Ideas

When—not if—God speaks to you through the Bible, highlight the verse(s). Date your entry, describe the situation, and keep it as a testimony of how He reveals His will through Scripture. These reminders will be a treasure trove of answered prayers!

Journal

_____

_____

_____

_____

_____

_____

_____

journal

_____

_____

_____

_____

_____

_____

_____

_____

_____

_____

_____

_____

_____

_____

_____

_____

_____

_____

_____

_____

_____

_____

Hearing God

journal

_____

_____

_____

_____

_____

_____

_____

_____

_____

_____

_____

_____

_____

_____

_____

_____

_____

_____

_____

_____

_____

_____

_____

_____

_____

Hearing God

Serving

"Do nothing from selfish ambition or conceit, but in humility count others more significant than yourselves. Let each of you look not only to his own interests but also to the interests of others." ~ Philippians 2:3-4 (ESV)

Hello Friend,

Often, as moms, we get caught up in the mundaneness of everyday life, and find ourselves serving others out of obligation instead of love. I call this being on "mom autopilot." We move from breakfast to preschool pickup to elementary carpool line to dance lessons to basketball to midweek church to dinner to homework to bath to bedtime to repeat all over the next day. How radically would our family lives change if we committed to serve our families out of love instead of obligation? We need to slow down and really interact with the people that we know and love. If we truly served in love, our homes would become calmer, friendlier, and full of grace. Would you commit to serving your family with love rather than out of obligation, and see how it changes your family?

I hope that you are finding value in service to others, not only in your home, but also in your community as well. Do you currently spend time serving others? A great place to get started is in your church home. Head to the church office and see what areas of ministry need a helping hand. Another great way to find a place to serve is to ask a friend. Use your mom network to identify a local need and creatively meet that need.

When you find yourself weary, take refuge in 2 Thessalonians 3:13, "And as for you, brothers and sisters, never tire of doing what is good."

So, dear friend, hold fast to that thought while you serve Jesus and others.

Love,
Leslie Leonard and the Help Club For Moms Team

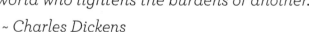
No one is useless in this world who lightens the burdens of another.
~ Charles Dickens

Mom Tips

"I am the vine; you are the branches. If you remain in me and I in you, you will bear much fruit..." ~ John 15:5

The Wise Woman Builds Her Spirit

- Listen to a Help Club for Moms video from our Facebook page and journal about what you learned. Be sure to grab a load of laundry to fold as you listen.

- Meditate on Acts 1:8. Jesus promises us the Holy Spirit will give us power and ability to witness. Ask the Lord for a fresh anointing and boldness to share the gospel with others.

The Wise Woman Loves Her Husband

- Give your husband a massage. It could be a quick 5-minute shoulder or foot rub. Perhaps, after the kids are put to bed, you could treat him to a longer, fancier massage with massage oil and relaxing music.

- Ask your mother-in-law or husband what meal was considered special when he was growing up. Plan to surprise him with it!

The Wise Woman Loves Her Children

- Every morning this week, wake up in the morning for your children instead of to your children. There is a difference. Set an alarm if you need to, to ensure that you wake up before your children. Smile and greet your family with love and remind them that this is the day that the Lord has made and we should rejoice.

- Read your children the story of the little boy who gave two fish and five pieces of bread when asked by Jesus' disciples (John 6:1-15). Talk about how the little boy had the generous heart of a servant and how Jesus used his gift to perform a miracle! Jesus can do big things through your children if they choose to serve Him!

The Wise Woman Cares For Her Home

- Get in the habit of making a "6 Most Important" list before you go to bed. Ask God for what He thinks are your most important tasks for the next day, and write down the top six. Cross them off during the day as you accomplish them.

- Pray that God will fill your heart with joy this week as you serve your family and care for your home. Don't underestimate the impact a mother's joyful service has for God's kingdom. Feel blessed in your special calling this week!

"The first question which the priest and the Levite asked was: 'If I stop to help this man, what will happen to me?' But the good Samaritan reversed the question: 'If I do not stop to help this man, what will happen to him?'"
~ Martin Luther King Jr.

- Call your prayer partner for your 10-minute prayer call. Keep trying to connect until you get to pray together. This tiny habit of praying with a friend regularly will truly change your life!

- This is the day that the Lord has made! Open up your Bible and journal and prepare your heart to meet Jesus. He wants you to draw near to Him, and He is eager to hear your prayers.

- Please read Romans 12:9-13. Wow! These powerful verses are convicting, yet they represent a beautiful commission and declaration.

Sacrificial Serving with Your Children

By: Rachel Jones

I absolutely love serving with my kids! Cherished memories are made, their hearts are forever impacted, and the people we are serving experience true joy and compassion that can only come from one source—Jesus Christ. Jesus Christ himself was the ultimate role model and sacrificial servant. Matthew 20:28 says, "Just as the Son of Man did not come to be served, but to serve..." Serving was one of His main missions when he was here on Earth! Showering love and compassion on those in need was displayed so well for us by the Son of Man. His actions showed us that sacrificial serving is one of the most powerful ways to change lives forever for the Kingdom.

I used to work for Young Life, and during that season, my three girls and I spent every Thursday from 9:00 am until 2:00 pm serving hundreds of high school students grilled cheese sandwiches for lunch. We prepped the sandwiches, cooked them, served them, then we sat and fellowshipped with the students, and finally, we spent the end of our time cleaning up. Eeekk! It was truly exhausting. And if I can be honest, a lot of Thursday mornings, I would wake up frustrated and completely not in the mood to go.

However, the most beautiful and rewarding part of those years was seeing my girls thrive in their duties, and most importantly, thrive spiritually. It was strenuous work, but they also reaped the benefits. I remember talking openly with them about how we, as Christ followers, are called to serve. I explained 1 Peter 4:10 to them and told them they were being "faithful stewards of God's grace." My children were able to see their mother praying with high school students. They witnessed teenagers who were depressed, insecure, and unable to fill the voids in their hearts. I was able to share the Gospel with my own three daughters from all of this.

Serving with my children prompted amazing discussions and helped shape my girls' world views. Also, those memories are some of the most powerful and tangible examples for my daughters to know and feel with all certainty how much of a need there is for Jesus. They saw with their own eyes that God is the only source of true happiness!

This thought of serving with your little children may seem daunting, but it doesn't have to be. I realize I had a job that was very conducive to serving; but serving can really happen everywhere, even in the smallest moments! Serving simply boils down to love: showing love, modeling love, and doing it freely and humbly, even when no one is noticing. Galatians 5:13, "You, my brothers and sisters, were called to be free. But do not use your freedom to indulge the flesh; rather, serve one another humbly in love."

Questions to Ponder

- Has serving ever impacted your family in the past? If it's been awhile, why did you stop...or why did it fall off your schedule?

- Thinking about your own family and its dynamics, how would serving impact all of you?

- Does the thought of serving with your kids delight you or terrify you? Honestly, I know as a mom with little children, it can be so hard. I simply want to challenge your way of thinking about serving. How can your own heart become softer toward it?

Faith-Filled Ideas

Start serving alongside your children! Pray to make it a priority to introduce an area of being a servant into your routine with your kids. Also, use this opportunity to share with your kids some of the verses I mentioned and teach them that Jesus loved to serve! Lastly, pray for your children's hearts to soften toward others and for them to eventually see opportunities to serve all on their own. Here are some easy ways to serve with your children:

- You can watch your friend's children when she has an appointment. Your children will have to sacrifice alongside you as they share their toys and play with these kids.

- Offer to give a neighbor kid a ride to school since you are driving there already. Your kids may have to wake up a few minutes earlier now to accommodate this new schedule.

- Bring a meal to a new mom. Have your kids help prepare the meal, and pray for the family as you are driving the meal to them.

_____

_____

_____

_____

_____

journal

_____
_____
_____
_____
_____
_____
_____
_____
_____
_____
_____
_____
_____
_____
_____
_____
_____
_____
_____
_____
_____
_____
_____
_____
_____
_____
_____
_____

Serving

> "If you are pleased with me, teach me your ways so I may know you and continue to find favor with you. Remember that this nation is your people." The Lord replied, "My Presence will go with you, and I will give you rest."
>
> ~ Exodus 33:13-14

"Let us think often that our only business in this life is to please God. Perhaps all besides is but folly and vanity."
~ Brother Lawrence

- Welcome, friend. Invite the Holy Spirit to fill you today; ask for new revelations and insights as we take a little Old Testament journey in Exodus. If you're unfamiliar with the Israelite Exodus, I highly encourage you to read through the first 20 chapters over the next few weeks. Each narrative is an incredible testament to the impact of obedience, the painful consequences of disobedience, and God's sovereign power and victorious nature. Today, read Exodus 33.

When God Calls Us to Serve

By: Rebekah Measmer

Moses was the great Hebrew-born prince of Egypt who fled his country in fear and returned as God's mouthpiece to liberate the Israelites and guide them into the Promised Land. Moses was the Old Testament poster boy for sacrificially serving God's people day after day. In Exodus 3, Moses did not believe he was the right man for the job, but God did. And despite Moses' doubts, he obeyed. He followed God's direction wherever it led—right into the heart of the most powerful nation on earth, where he happened to be wanted for murder. That's true trust and obedience!

The good news is that God did not send him alone. Moses' brother Aaron was sent by God to meet up with him before they confronted Pharaoh. Fast forward through discouragement, plagues, a dramatic escape through the parting of the Red Sea (Exodus 14), and the desolation of the Egyptian army, to a wilderness with over one million people in his care and no food or water. Moses had a huge responsibility! But, remember, he wasn't alone. God was with him every step of the way, and God continued to provide all that was needed as Moses' daunting tasks increased—and they did increase!

With Egypt behind them and the Promised Land ahead, the Israelites were every bit as human as we and our children are, and they complained. They complained about a lack of food. They complained about a lack of water. They complained about neighborly disputes. Poor Moses did not have enough hours in the day for all that was asked of him, so God used the wisdom of Jethro, Moses' father-in-law, to help him appoint other leaders to serve the many needs of this great nation of people (Exodus 18).

About this time, a young man named Joshua also came on the scene as Moses' aid and military commander. Joshua, dutifully serving Moses, accompanied him to Mount Sinai and the Tent of Meeting which were two of the key places that Moses heard from God. Exodus 33:11 says, "The Lord would speak to Moses face to face, as one speaks to a friend. Then Moses would return to the camp, but his young aide Joshua son of Nun did not leave the tent." Hmm. Joshua did not leave the

Serving

tent. No ink is wasted in the Scriptures. Every word and line holds significance. Joshua remained in the presence of Almighty God even after his mentor returned to business. After Moses' death, God chose Joshua to lead His people because he not only served, but he also lingered.

Friend, there are so many rich truths in this incredible history of God's provision and faithfulness:

1. God does not call the "equipped," He equips the "called." All He requires is trust and obedience.

2. God never sends us alone. He is always with us, and he will provide help and wisdom for us along the way.

3. Linger: linger in the Lord's presence each day as He calls you to serve, devotedly completing the tasks that He has set before you to do.

Questions to Ponder

• Are you trusting that God chose you specifically and placed you strategically where you are, because no other woman can fulfill the individual calling He has placed on you as a woman, wife, mother, friend, etc., or are you doubting God's ability to choose the right person for the job?

• Are there areas in your life where you are not walking in obedience to His call to serve because of fear or busyness with your own agenda?

• As you are serving your family and others God has placed in your path, are you seeking wisdom from other spirit-filled believers and accepting help from the people God has sent your way, or are you pridefully trying to do everything on your own?

• How much time are you spending truly "lingering" with God each day in worship, prayer, and Bible study?

Faith-Filled Ideas

Pray for God to direct your steps and highlight areas where He has called you to serve. Whether you are called to serve as a wife and mother at home, a Sunday school teacher, a counselor, a PTA member, or a little bit of each, you are called to lovingly serve God's children *wherever* you are! If no obvious answer is apparent at this time, keep serving where you are now!

Read Exodus with your children using a children's illustrated story Bible if you have one. Discuss the way Moses and Aaron (and later Joshua) served God's people so faithfully, despite the difficulties and their personal fears. Contrast God's provision for their obedience with Pharaoh's hard-hearted disobedience. Which heart attitude brought protection and blessing, obedience or disobedience? God wants each of us to have hearts that are soft toward Him! When our hearts are soft toward our Father, we long to please Him each day by walking in obedience to Him and serving those around us!

Joshua 24:14, "Now fear the LORD and serve him with all faithfulness."

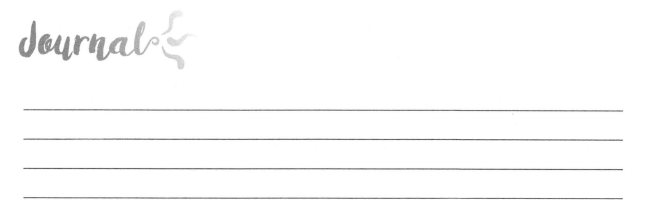

Serving

Journal

Serving

> **"** None of you should look out just for your own good.
> Each of you should also look out for the good of others. **"**
>
> ~ Philippians 2:4 (NIrV)

"What does love look like? It has the hands to help others. It has the feet to hasten to the poor and needy. It has eyes to see misery and want. It has the ears to hear the sighs and sorrows of man. That is what love looks like."
~ St. Augustine

- Hello dear mama! Find a comfortable place to sit, and bring a drink, a pen, and your Bible. Ask the Lord to speak to you today.

- Read Philippians chapter 2, and highlight verse 4.

- Read and meditate on Matthew 25:40, "Truly I tell you, whatever you did for one of the least of these brothers and sisters of mine, you did for me!"

- Read Ephesians 2:1-10, and write verse 10 in your journal.

Can You Lend a Hand?

By: Kathryn Egly

In elementary school, I wrote a story called, "The Entire City Lends a Hand!" I found this old story as I was going through a box of some special things my mom had saved for me. The title of this story has a new meaning to me as an adult. What if each of us really did "lend a hand" to help our cities? Imagine how much better the world could be if we all committed to making it a little bit better.

If you are a mom with young children, you may think you do not have the capacity for doing anything outside of your own home. And this may be true for a season. For instance, for a few months after I had each baby, I would take time off from serving because of pure exhaustion and learning our new "normal." After I had some time to adjust, I'd get plugged into serving somewhere! Serving helps us as individuals thrive, and it also blesses the people and organizations where we serve! Whether it's welcoming families into your church, bringing your children with you to serve the homeless in your community, or giving back by serving in the children's ministry where your children are loved and taught each week—most of us can do something. If each person does a little, no one has to do a lot!

Did you know that research proves that serving is one of the best ways to grow spiritually? I know when I'm leading something, it challenges me to study, learn, and pray! I'm no longer sitting on the sidelines, I'm in the game and need to prepare and train.

Ask God where you can be a blessing in your city. Where can you "lend a hand?" Is there a homeless shelter that could use some food, as well as people to serve that food? Is your local church asking for volunteers?

God is so good in that He will bless you when you are a blessing to others. When you invest in others, you are laying up an eternal investment for yourself. I'm forever grateful for the men and women who invested in me. It changed the trajectory of my life, and I'm writing this today because some men and women served in my local church, welcomed me, and reminded me that God loves me and has a good plan for my life. I look forward to thanking them one day in heaven!

Serving

"What do YOU have to offer? More than you probably think. You have the gifts and talents you were born with. The passion that inspires you. The blessing of education. The skills you've honed as you've worked at home or in the marketplace. The life experiences that have matured you. The pain that has deepened you. The love that spills from God's heart into yours." – Bill Hybels

Questions to Ponder

• How has your life been blessed because others have served you?

• Could you create space in your life to serve others?

• Could you gather supplies to donate to a ministry that feeds the needy in your community?

Faith-Filled Ideas

Ask the Holy Spirit to show you how you might be able to "lend a hand."

Reach out to someone this week and let them know you'd like to serve. Most churches and organizations will work with your schedule as a busy mom.

Journal

_____

_____

_____

_____

_____

_____

_____

_____

_____

_____

_____

_____

_____

_____

_____

_____

_____

_____

Serving

> "After that, he poured water into a basin and began to wash his disciples' feet, drying them with the towel that was wrapped around him... 'Now that I, your Lord and Teacher, have washed your feet, you also should wash one another's feet. I have set you an example that you should do as I have done for you. Very truly I tell you, no servant is greater than his master, nor is a messenger greater than the one who sent him. Now that you know these things, do these things, you will be blessed if you do them.'
>
> ~ John 13:5, 14-17

"The priorities and intentions—the heart and inner attitudes—of disciples are forever the same. In the heart of a disciple, there is a desire and there is a decision or settled intent. The disciple of Christ desires above all else to be like Him"
~ Dallas Willard

• Read John 13. Then write John 13:15-17 in your journal.

A Servant's Heart

By: Lauraine Bailey

When I first began spending time in God's Word, I heard the concept of a servant's heart. The more time I spent in God's Word, the more convinced I became that God valued a servant's heart. As I grew more and more in love with God, I wanted to please Him and obey Him. I read in the Bible that one of the last things Jesus did before He suffered on the cross for me was to take on the role of a servant and, in humility, chose to wash the dirty, stinky feet of His disciples.

Fast-forward to today: I know I want to be like Jesus, and as a mother, I want to do everything I can to encourage my children to be like Him. I feel so convicted that having a servant's heart is an integral part of my walk with the Lord. In a culture where entitlement is rampant, a servant's heart can combat that natural inner desire to be catered to, waited on, spoiled, and indulged.

When I have the privilege to serve, I am deeply blessed. I was once told that it was a privilege to serve, not a right. That stirred my heart. I long for my family to serve together, minister, offer hospitality, be kind, encourage others, work together, and be available to serve daily as opportunities arise. Even when my children were young, I encouraged them to think of others and how they could bless them. When my children reached the seventh grade, I told each of them that they had been served for so many years by the church, and now it was time for them to minister and give back. I asked them to pray about it and see where God would have them serve. As a result, my daughters now serve the toddlers. My sons serve 6th-grade boys on Sunday mornings. I rock babies. I also encourage my family to serve at a ministry my daughter is involved with. There, we tutor, mentor, build relationships, and share Christ. I pray that I model a servant's heart. My kids and I continue to change from the inside out when we serve and minister. Serving helps us to become more like Christ. We start out hoping to bless others, but often, we are the ones who end up being blessed. In fact, after serving in Mexico on a mission trip as a family, my kids told

Serving

me that it was better than going to Disney World. I want them to experience the joy of walking in obedience, humbly serving, and putting others first.

My prayer is that God will continually show me how to be kind to whomever He places in my path. He frequently amazes me with what He shows me. I know God desires us to be His hands and feet, and I know that what He calls us to do, He will equip us to do. Jesus perfectly modeled walking closely in relationship with His Father: listening, being attentive to those in His path, sensing their needs, and then serving and loving the souls He encountered.

Questions to Ponder

- Are you modeling a servant's heart?
- Are you asking God to help you to be attentive and sensitive to the needs of those in front of you?
- Are you encouraging your children to have a servant's heart?
- Are you praying and asking God to open your eyes to opportunities where your family can serve together?

Faith-Filled Ideas

Call the church and ask for ideas, ministry needs, or the names of families that might need some extra encouragement.

Consider mentoring together, as a family. Perhaps there is a child who needs some extra love and encouragement in your community.

Ask your family if they could pray and look for ways in which your family could be a blessing. Then make a list of ways to bless (for example, help a single mom with childcare, make cards for a nursing home, mow a neighbors yard, make a meal or cookies, etc.).

Journal

_____

_____

_____

_____

_____

_____

_____

_____

_____

_____

_____

journal

_____

_____

_____

_____

_____

_____

_____

_____

_____

_____

_____

_____

_____

_____

_____

_____

_____

_____

_____

_____

_____

_____

_____

_____

Serving

Dearest Mama, we are embarking on a busy season of serving <sigh>. I particularly love this time of year and all the entertaining that goes along with the upcoming holidays; however, I know that not everyone has the same feelings about serving and entertaining that I do. Serving is one of those things that we either enjoy or that we ask the Lord for perseverance for. We are all called to serve in one capacity or another, whether it is in your church body or on your HOA or PTA committee.

Cooking just happens to be a passion of mine. As a service to others, I make meals and deliver them to new moms or to those who are sick or having surgery. I feel called to this service, and find it is fulfilling to love on those who are in a time of need. This simple slow cooker recipe is comfort food at its best! It's simple and delicious! I hope you make it for your family on a cold winter's night, and maybe you will make a little extra to share with someone else as well. It is sure to warm spirit, body, and soul.

SAUSAGE TORTELLINI SOUP

By: Rae-Ellen Sanders

Ingredients:

- 1 bag of frozen cheese tortellini
- 1 bag of fresh spinach (not frozen)
- 2 (14.5 ounce) cans of regular Rotel diced tomatoes—undrained
- 1 block of Philadelphia cream cheese
- 1 pound of ground Italian sausage
- 4 cups of chicken broth
- 1 teaspoon Italian seasoning

Directions:

1. Brown the sausage in a skillet on the stovetop until cooked and crumbled. Drain.

2. Add the sausage, 2 cans of tomatoes, broth, and cream cheese to a slow cooker. Stir to combine.

3. Cook in the slow cooker on low for 4-6 hours, stirring twice during cooking.

4. Add the tortellini and spinach in the last 30 minutes of cooking time, and cook until tender.

   Note: My family of seven uses 2 bags of tortellini, and ultimately, the soup is absorbed so much that it becomes Sausage Tortellini Stew. Double all the ingredients to make enough to share.

Thanksgiving

Precious Mom,

When I think about Thanksgiving, two words come to mind: Bountiful harvest. Bountiful means a large or abundant quantity. Harvest is the product or result of an action.

Often, we highlight Thanksgiving as a one-day affair inviting family and friends over, and adorning our tables with wonderful delicacies and succulent dishes. It is wonderful, but the day comes and goes by so quickly, and we easily forget the importance of staying thankful all year long. We have so much to thank God for!

This year, God is stirring inside me as I meditate on the many blessings He has bestowed upon me—they are too numerous to count! I want to exercise gratefulness daily, so much so that my children notice. I want them to know I would not be who I am, were it not for God's abundant blessings, and my children are one of the main dishes! All the other sides are great, but they are the most flavorful, colorful ones of all! They are a large part of my harvest and I want them to live thankfully, too.

As you lovingly parent, faithfully investing in your kids, don't forget that little things lead to big things. A bountiful harvest awaits in your not-too-distant future if you patiently continue with the small things. Your children are growing and you only have a few short years to make the most of every day.

We do our very, very best when we keep the blessings God has given us in front of us, moment by moment. Our hearts stay humble and soft, and our children notice. Thank God in all things because He's the One who is worthy to be praised!

Blessings to you this Thanksgiving,
Mari Jo Mast and the Help Club For Moms Team

Gratitude is the healthiest of all human emotions.
The more you express gratitude for what you have,
the more likely you will have even more to express gratitude for.
~ Zig Ziglar

"I am the vine; you are the branches. If you remain in me and I in you, you will bear much fruit..." ~ John 15:5

The Wise Woman Builds Her Spirit

- Continue writing in your gratitude journal and start each day with a grateful heart. Write five blessings each day this week.
- Memorize Psalm 107:1. What a great verse to remind us to have a thankful heart!

The Wise Woman Loves Her Husband

- Plan a night to sit with your husband after your children have gone to bed. Be sure to tell him what you appreciate and admire about him.
- If your husband likes sports, watch a game with him. Show interest and excitement for his team.

The Wise Woman Loves Her Children

- Create a Thanksgiving journal that can be added to each year. Pass it around the table each year at Thanksgiving and have your guests record what they are thankful for. This makes beautiful "thankful" memories for years to come!
- Make "turkey tickets" for Thanksgiving dinner. Prepare long strips of paper and give one to each of your children the day before Thanksgiving. Ask them to write down all of their blessings, fun memories from the past year, and things they can say "thank you" to God for. They must bring the turkey ticket to the table filled out in order to receive their Thanksgiving meal. Sharing what is written on the turkey tickets makes for a fun family tradition!

The Wise Woman Cares For Her Home

- Clean out your refrigerator to prepare for Thanksgiving leftovers.
- Burn holiday candles, the yummy ones; cinnamon apple, oatmeal cookie, etc. The scent helps create an atmosphere of a homey refuge.

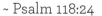 The Lord has done it this very day; let us rejoice today and be glad.
~ Psalm 118:24

"Your big picture will never be a masterpiece if you ignore the tiny brushstrokes."
~ Andy Andrews

- Call your prayer partner for your 10-minute prayer call. Keep it short but meaningful. Pray for your Thanksgiving week—for all of your preparations and interactions with your family and friends to be blessed.

- Welcome, daughter of the Most High God! Gather your favorite beverage, your journal, and your Bible, sit at the feet of our mighty God and soak in what He has for your heart today.

- Read Psalm 118, and write Psalm 118:24 in your journal.

Thanksgiving Is a Time of Reflected Blessings

By: Pam Mays

As we enter this season of Thanksgiving, stop for a moment and ponder the blessings the Lord has given you this year. Surely, there were changes and challenges too, but let's focus on the blessings.

Our blessings this year came in the form of a job transfer. My teenagers and I chose to stay in Florida while my husband worked out of state for the majority of the year. And just as we were all to reunite in another state, he received a different job offer in Florida. Even though this job offered less money, the other opportunities—like being 10 minutes from the Gulf of Mexico—far outweighed the loss of income. Now, I do not take enough time to enjoy this great blessing, but on occasion, it is wonderful to drive out to the ocean and watch the waves in the early morning or at sunset and to soak in God's amazing creation. Sometimes God changes things to bring greater blessings. Is there something that was challenging in your life this year that has brought blessings?

The song "This is the Day" by Les Garrett comes to mind as I think about the blessings God has brought this year. I love the second verse that reminds us that we are the sons and daughters of the living God, Creator of the universe! Let's rejoice that God chose each of us to be His!

This is the Day

This is the day, this is the day.
That the Lord has made, that the Lord has made.
We will rejoice, we will rejoice,
And be glad in it, and be glad in it.
This is the day that the Lord has made.
We will rejoice and be glad in it.
This is the day, this is the day
That the Lord has made.

We are the sons, we are the sons,
Of the living God, of the living God.
We will rejoice, we will rejoice,
And be glad in Him, and be glad in Him.
We are the sons of the living God.
We will rejoice and be glad in Him.
We are the sons, we are the sons
Of the living God.

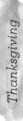

Take a few moments this morning and think of the blessings that have come from your challenges this year.

Questions to Ponder

· Was there something that was challenging this year in your life that has brought blessings?

Faith-Filled Ideas

Write in your journal a change or challenge God brought this year.

Now take some time to think about and write the blessings that have come from this change or challenge. If there is not a blessing yet, think of what the blessing or blessings could be.

Lastly, think of a way you can be a blessing today. How can you bless someone in your sphere of influence? It could be your husband, your children, or a simple text to a friend letting them know you are thinking about them and wishing them a wonderful day.

Journal

_____

_____

_____

_____

_____

_____

_____

_____

_____

_____

_____

_____

_____

_____

_____

_____

_____

> 66 To everything there is a season,
> A time for every purpose under heaven. 99
> ~ Ecclesiastes 3:1 (NKJV)

"A thankful heart is one of the primary identifying characteristics of a believer. It stands in stark contrast to pride, selfishness, and worry. And it helps fortify the believer's trust in the Lord and reliance of His provision, even in the toughest times. No matter how choppy the seas become, a believer's heart is buoyed by constant praise and gratefulness to the Lord."
~ John Mac Arthur

- "Abide" means to remain. Take a deep breath and clear your mind. If necessary, set a timer for five minutes to create a mood of stillness.

- Read Ecclesiastes 3. What verse represents your life today?

- Reflect on this time in your life and write down thoughts in your journal

- During your prayer time, ask the Lord to put a godly, older woman in your life as a mentor.

Embrace this Moment in Time

By: Melissa Lain

Oh, how lovely is fall: a change in season, the glow of golden light casting its warmth on all that it touches. The joy of entering this time brings us the great anticipation of the celebration of Thanksgiving and its charm! Since it is my personal favorite time of year, our house transforms into a harvest of warmth, with pumpkin scents and festive florals and fabrics. In the past, I packed my kids' lunches with seasonal napkins and tasty festive treats. Now, as they return home from college, we all share in the memories that flood back from fall seasons of the past!

My perspective of truly abiding took root years ago while sharing a parenting issue with a mentor. She recommended that we savor the phases of struggle with our child, whether, in happy or frustrating chapters of parenting, those times equip us to rejoice in this daily grind.

Living on the Texas Gulf Coast has fed into our anxiety when awaiting the shift to the fall season. The season ushers in family, memories, and an attitude of gratitude that prepares us for the embracing of loved ones. Unfortunately, individuals rush through Thanksgiving to put trees & lights up in preparation for Christmas, all the while missing the opportunity to abide in the consciousness of this point in time.

"Such a time as this…" Esther 4:14. Moms, become aware and present. Time vanishes, the stage of life you exist in now, most likely, will never happen again. Little hands and feet to clean, bottoms to wipe… gone. Stop for a moment and reap the beauty of the mundane, the routine, because in the blink of an eye, dear one, it is gone! God has given you a calling, cherished mother and wife, to set the tone, to practice and evolve into a role model of all things good in your home. The impressionable young lives you have an impact on every day are watching. When you look back on these days, these precious crazy moments in time, how do you want to be remembered?

How often do you pause, busy mom, in your daily routine to reflect on the riches of "this moment?"

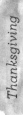

We rush from one event to the next only to forfeit the blessing of what that occasion or reality offers. Why don't we remain in the now, just for today?

During this Thanksgiving holiday, practice embracing all things dear: health, homes, family, and traditions, without rushing or expectations. Expose yourself to the pleasure of the here and now (Psalm 46:10)!

> "The remarkable thing is, we have a choice every day regarding the attitude we will embrace for that day." - Charles R. Swindoll

Dear one, apply this truth in every area of life. As a child of the Almighty God, where you are, right now, is no coincidence!

Questions to Ponder

• Do you have a heart full of gratitude for this time, this place?

• What does your sweet Savior desire from you?

Faith-Filled Ideas

Write in your journal: how you will escape the pressure to rush, list the traditions you want to take place during this holiday, prioritize, and prepare.

You will make this a beautiful and memorable Thanksgiving!

Journal

_____

_____

_____

_____

_____

_____

_____

_____

_____

_____

_____

_____

_____

> ❝ Do not be anxious about anything, but in everything, by prayer and supplication, with thanksgiving let your requests be made known to God. ❞
>
> ~ Philippians 4:6 (ESV)

"When joy and prayer are married, their first born child is gratitude."
~ Charles Spurgeon

- Take some time out of your busy preparations for the holidays to sit down with the Lord for a time of thanksgiving and prayer. Read through Philippians 4:4-8 and meditate on God's promises to you and also on what He asks you to do. He promises you peace!

In Everything Give Thanks!

By: Carmen Brown

I love the fall! The crispness in the air, the falling leaves, and the pumpkins arriving in stores all leave me in excited anticipation for the entire holiday season! I enjoy the simplicity of the good food and fellowship that Thanksgiving brings. But in all of this, there are a lot of expectations that can leave a Mama feeling tired, overwhelmed, and even anxious. That is why I love our verse for today! It says "Do not be anxious about anything, but in every situation, by prayer and petition, with thanksgiving, present your requests to God" (Philippians 4:6-7).

Do not be anxious about anything? Does that feel impossible to you? Without the fullness of Christ in you, it is impossible. But as Matthew 19:26 says,"with God *all* things are possible." This verse does not simply tell you not to be anxious. Instead of stewing in anxiety, it tells you to pray with thanksgiving about every situation. Are you facing seemingly impossible situations with family coming into town, or are you struggling financially and anxiously wondering how you are going to make the holidays special this year? Remember to focus on thanking the Lord for the blessings of family and the things that you do have. Ask Him to help you with those things that are causing anxiety. He will give you a new perspective! If you can't find any thanksgiving in your heart, ask Him for that too! He will answer you! When you are feeling anxious, pray with thanksgiving!

1 Thessalonians 5:18 (ESV) says, "Rejoice always, pray without ceasing, give thanks in all circumstances; for this is the will of God in Christ Jesus for you." Giving thanks in all circumstances is another seemingly impossible task without God. But this verse says that it is God's will for you, in Christ Jesus! In Christ, we can face all of the holiday preparations and life expectations with thanksgiving. But we can't set Jesus aside. We need to take time to sit quietly at Jesus' feet both in solitude and in the middle of our tasks to focus on Him and seek Him for strength and for a thankful heart. Jesus told Martha when she was getting flustered and upset about all that she had to get done, "Mary has chosen the better part and it will not be taken from her" (Luke 10:42). Your heart can be in a place of rest and gratitude as you fill up with His love and care for you. Then you can go forth in thanksgiving, doing all that is required of you!

That heart of thankfulness will come as you pray without ceasing. Pray over your preparations. Pray while you bake and cook and clean for the upcoming festivities. Put Jesus at the central focus of all that you are doing, and you will find peace. But also make sure that you are not taking on more than is required of you. Seek the Lord for what He wants you to do. Let go of any traditions and expectations that are stealing your joy. And as you practice more constant prayer and thanksgiving, Philippians 4:7 (ESV) promises that "the peace of God, which surpasses all understanding will guard your hearts and your minds in Christ Jesus."

My prayer for you this Thanksgiving and as you head into the holiday season comes from a quote by Charles Spurgeon, "Let gratitude be awakened; let humility be deepened; let love be quickened."

Questions to Ponder

- Are you taking on too much to make Thanksgiving and the upcoming holidays "perfect" for everyone? Do not keep a tradition for tradition's sake. If it is becoming burdensome, it is alright to let some traditions go and maybe make a few new, simpler ones! As Proverbs 17:1 (NLT) says, "Better a dry crust eaten in peace than a house filled with feasting—and conflict."

- How can you "sit at Jesus' feet" as you make preparations? What can you do to remind yourself to pray without ceasing and to not be anxious about anything but instead pray, with thankfulness in your heart?

Faith-Filled Ideas

Start a thanksgiving basket on your dining table: have your family write down things that they are thankful for and put these into the basket. Keep thankfulness at the center of your home!

Put these verses from Philippians somewhere in your kitchen to remind you what to do when anxiety begins to take over during all of your preparations or your time with family.

Journal

_____

_____

_____

_____

_____

_____

_____

_____

_____

_____

_____

_____

Do you ever wonder what to do with all those turkey leftovers at Thanksgiving? After a heavy Thanksgiving dinner with all the gravies and rich dishes, my husband likes to have something light. And for a change in flavor, I learned to get creative with the abundance of leftover turkey. I started turning it into a version of chicken (or turkey in this case) tortilla soup. As a bonus, if you save the turkey carcass, you can simply make your own broth as the base for this soup. This is not only cost-effective but also very healthy for you. If you are nervous about making your own broth, don't worry—boxed broth works great too! When you don't have an abundance of turkey, regular chicken breasts will work great as well.

LEFTOVER TURKEY TORTILLA SOUP
(And How to Make Homemade Broth and Slow Cooker Black Beans)
By: Brandi Carson

Ingredients:

Olive oil

1 large, or 2 medium onions, diced

2-3 garlic cloves, minced

1 large red bell pepper, diced

4 ounce can of diced green chiles

2 cups of salsa or 1 can of Rotel tomatoes with green chiles

1 (10-ounce) bag of frozen corn

2 cans of black beans, drained or 2-3 cups homemade easy peasy crockpot black beans (*recipe below*)

3-4 cups of leftover turkey (or chicken), diced

96 ounces of chicken (or homemade turkey) broth

⅓ cup homemade taco seasoning or 1 package taco seasoning

10 corn tortillas, finely diced

Directions:

1. Heat a large stockpot or Dutch oven to medium heat. Drizzle pot generously with olive oil and sauté garlic for a minute until aromatic.

2. Add onions and bell peppers, and sauté until tender.

3. Add green chile, salsa, corn, black beans, turkey (or chicken), broth, and taco seasoning. Stir to mix well, increase the heat to medium-high, and bring to a boil.

4. Once the soup is at a boil, add finely diced corn tortillas. The corn tortillas will break down and help to thicken the soup. Stir to combine and cover. Simmer until the corn tortillas are broken down and the soup has thickened, stirring occasionally.

5. Serve with cheese, sour cream, salsa, and grilled tortillas or tortilla chips.

HOMEMADE TURKEY (OR CHICKEN) BROTH

Ingredients:

Turkey carcass

1 large or 2 small onions, coarsely chopped

3-4 carrots, coarsely chopped

3-4 stalks of celery, coarsely chopped

Salt and pepper to taste, be generous

Note: If you don't have any extra vegetables on hand, you can make broth with just the bones, water, salt, and pepper.

Directions:

1. Place all ingredients in a stockpot and cover with water, making sure the carcass is submerged by a few inches. Bring to a boil.

2. Simmer on medium-high heat, covered for several hours. Add water if needed. The longer the broth cooks, the richer and more nutritious it will be.

3. Strain broth and let cool.

   Note: If you have a smaller turkey or are making chicken broth, you can even use a slow cooker. Add all the ingredients, cover with water, and season generously with salt and pepper. Cook on high heat for 8-10 hours, keeping the water level at the top of the cooker.

EASY PEASY SLOW COOKER BLACK BEANS

Ingredients:

1 (16-ounce) bag of dried black beans

⅓ cup homemade taco seasoning or 1 package taco seasoning

1 (4-ounce) can of green chiles

Directions:

1. Rinse black beans and check for any stones.

2. Add black beans, taco seasoning, and green chiles to slow cooker. Fill with water, making sure that the beans are submerged by a few inches. Cook on high for 6-8 hours or on low for 10-12.

3. Ready to serve.

   Note: This makes more than needed for the recipe, so you can freeze leftovers in individual containers or freezer bags. I frequently make extra to have on hand and ready to use as a side dish or for other recipes.

Christmas
~ Week One ~

Hi Mama,

I hope you had a blessed Thanksgiving, filled with gratitude. We have four weeks of encouraging studies ahead to help prepare our hearts for a joyful Christmas season. Here at the Help Club for Moms, our goal as God-honoring wives and mothers is to be intentional in our attitudes, actions and words; its importance cannot be overstated. So let's be mindful to make choices that will inspire worship and celebration in our homes this Christmas season.

Representing and following Jesus in a broken world takes every ounce of our attention and planning, especially during Christmas time. Consumerism wants to flash and parade toys and Santa Claus at every turn. As Christian moms, we want to fervently plant seeds of faith into our little ones' hearts so they will understand that Christmas is so much more than presents and twinkle lights.

We can all enjoy the excitement of Christmas traditions while putting Christ in the center of Christmas! One way to incorporate Christ is through worship. In the midst of decorating, baking, and wrapping presents, we can tune our hearts to the words of faith-filled Christmas hymns. Print the words to your favorite hymns, meditate on them, and sing them with your family. I particularly love the idea of 30 Christmas Acts of Giving. Children experience the joy of giving and doing something nice for someone else every day of the month. I hope to implement it this year. I want my children to learn to love others well. Romans 12:9-10 (NLT) teaches us, "Don't just pretend to love others. Really love them. Hate what is wrong. Hold tightly to what is good. Love each other with genuine affection, and take delight in honoring each other."

As we continue to meditate on the beauty of Jesus' birth, let's be intentional about seeking Him this Christmas!

Love & Blessings,
Rae-Ellen Sanders and the Help Club for Moms Team

> *When they had seen him, they spread the word concerning what had been told them about this child.*
>
> *~ Luke 2:17*

Mom Tips

*"I am the vine; you are the branches. If you remain
in me and I in you, you will bear much fruit..."* ~ John 15:5

The Wise Woman Builds Her Spirit

- Be sure to make time in your schedule for regular Bible study and prayer this Christmas season! Things can get really busy during the holidays, so time with God is more essential than ever to keep your sense of inner peace. Pray and ask God to help you focus on Him more than anything else, and for His help to be patient and to love your family well.

- Take a moment to give yourself a pedicure; paint your nails a festive color. Moms need to have fun, too!

The Wise Woman Loves Her Husband

- Lay under the Christmas tree together before you place presents under it. Look up at all the lights, and reflect on your past Christmases.

- Start a yearly tradition for you and your husband. Plan a quiet or festive date night, and make it a priority. Setting time aside to keep your marriage healthy during a potentially stressful time of year will help you view each other as partners. Here are some simple ideas: go out for dessert or tea, take a walk around the neighborhood to enjoy Christmas lights, go for a walk in the snow, or try ice skating together.

The Wise Woman Loves Her Children

- Keep Christmas music playing all month! Have spontaneous dance parties with your children! It will put your kids in a great mood and build musical Christmas memories in their hearts.

- Make a "Countdown to Christmas" Paper Chain out of red and green construction paper. Type the words to the Christmas story on slips of paper—staple or tape them to the garland. Have your child read the Scriptures each day. This is a fun, interactive decoration.

The Wise Woman Cares For Her Home

- Set up a hot cocoa station on your counter. Use pretty jars or containers and a tray to hold all of your hot cocoa fixings (cocoa, marshmallows, candy canes, etc.). Now you have everything at your fingertips for when your children come in and out of the cold. It is also fun for each child to occasionally make their own special treat!

- Make a gift-wrap organizer: purchase an under the bed organizer tote and fill with Christmas gift wrap, bags, tissue paper, gift tags, ribbon, tape, scissors, etc. You could even make one as a gift!

> Each of you should give what you have decided in your heart to give, not reluctantly or under compulsion, for God loves a cheerful giver.
>
> ~ 2 Corinthians 9:7

"For it is in giving that we receive."
~ Francis of Assisi

- Call your prayer partner today for your 10-minute prayer call.

- Time with your precious Savior is on the horizon. Silence your phone and find a quiet place. Get comfortable with your Bible, a pen and journal, and a warm drink.

- Please read 2 Corinthians 9:8-11 in your Bible. Copy verse 11 down in your journal or on an index card. Keep it close to you this week and share it with your children, too!

The Joy of Giving at Christmas

By: Rachel Jones

As parents, we love to bestow gifts upon our children. Seeing the joy on their faces is our gift. Children unanimously adore receiving gifts, and isn't it interesting how no one has to teach them how to enjoy the gifts they love and desire? Likewise, no one has to teach us how to give to our children. We love our families, so we give. Giving absolutely comes from an overflow of love from our hearts!

How do we share that overflow with our children? I think we have to focus on three things: Christ's unconditional love for us, His desire for us to love other people unconditionally, and that we have been given the greatest gift of all in Him. Through His love and His sacrifice, we have been guided towards generosity. Genuine, free giving, without regret, is an expression of thanksgiving to God! This can be an extremely difficult concept for young children to understand, but it is essential for us to lay the foundation of this principle down for them at an early age.

Proverbs 11:24-25 (ESV) says, "One gives freely, yet grows all the richer; another withholds what he should give, and only suffers want. Whoever brings blessing will be enriched, and one who waters will himself be watered." My children (ages 10, 8, 7, and 2) and I recently discussed these verses, and I explained to them that they simply mean the more we grasp and hoard, the more we need. Also, when we give freely and generously, we find that we're happier, healthier, and experience more blessings. Wow! All kids can comprehend that, and the tangible way to show them is to invite them to experience the joy of generosity firsthand.

Teaching our children to enjoy giving requires focus and attention. As parents, we have to first model the behavior in our actions and in how we speak. We need to live out what Jesus says in Acts 20:35, that "It is more blessed to give than to receive." As December and Christmas near, we should prayerfully emphasize the people in our lives and notice their needs. Our children will come alongside us and truly enjoy this process if we set a tone of happiness and sacrifice.

In our home, it always starts with a list. Bringing my children into the Christmas gift-giving planning and list-making is a fun day, especially when we do it with hot chocolate! We encourage them to consider who would enjoy what kind of present. My girls are then moved to think of other people first and foremost, and you will see Philippians 2:3-4 in action right before your eyes! "....but in humility consider others better than yourselves. Each of you should look not only to your own interests, but to the interests of others."

Once the presents are purchased, set up a wrapping station to get your kids in the festive and joyful spirit! I let my three girls wrap almost all of our extended family's presents and also handwrite the gift tags. It is always so fun for me to see them smiling throughout the whole process, but the best moment is when the presents are opened. Christmas day or Christmas Eve will no longer be consumed with your kids and their new toys. They will be thrilled to give, and their hearts will be in the right place for them to learn and hear from the Lord.

Questions to Ponder

• Search your own heart. How are you doing in the generosity department? Honestly, do you find that giving to others is a cheerful act or is it a chore to you?

• Answer this question with me: Lord, how can I make one simple change to model joyful giving to my children this Christmas?

Faith-Filled Ideas

If you have an elementary-aged child or older, assign them one relative that they are solely responsible for this Christmas, preferably a cousin or a close family friend's child because kids love buying and decorating/wrapping gifts for other kids! Encourage your child(ren) to pray for this person as they are planning their gift.

During the month of December, my girls and I focus on praying for our extended family. We pray they will feel loved, appreciated, and noticed this Christmas season. If you have non-Christian relatives, this is a fantastic opportunity to pray over the gift and card you made. Pray the Holy Spirit speaks to them through your gift. What a simple, yet powerful way to add prayer, thoughtfulness, and discipleship into gift giving!

Journal

_____

_____

_____

_____

_____

_____

_____

_____

Journal

_____
_____
_____
_____
_____
_____
_____
_____
_____
_____
_____
_____
_____
_____
_____
_____
_____
_____
_____
_____
_____
_____
_____
_____
_____
_____
_____
_____
_____
_____

Christmas ~ Week One ~ Day One

Christmas

"The Son of God became a man to enable men to become the sons of God."
~ C.S. Lewis

- Christmas is here! The celebration of Jesus' birth is upon us! Take time to be intentional with your Savior in these next weeks. This season is infinitely more meaningful when our hearts and minds are focused on Jesus!

- Read 1 John 4:9-18 and write verses 9-10 in your journal. This is the Christmas that God's love changes everything!

Fall in Love with Jesus this Christmas

By: Tara Davis

Sweet friend, I'm sure you have so much on your plate right now, and it is easy to be distracted by the glitz and glam of the Christmas season. The decorations are beautiful, the food is scrumptious, and it is such a pleasant time to make memories with your family. But wait! Do not exchange the celebration of the magnificent, glorious gift of our Savior for some pretty baubles, shopping trips, and endless Christmas to-do lists.

Clear away time this season. Say no to some activities, leave some décor in the boxes, and think about the traditions that really bring glory to God. What we are celebrating is *huge!* Christ came to change *everything*, and He is coming again soon (Hebrews 9:28)! He asks that we prepare our hearts for Him (1 Peter 1:13). And that preparation requires us to be still and consider what Jesus did for us two thousand years ago when He took the form, not simply of a man, but of a helpless baby at the mercy of the very people He came to save.

He took on the mantle of a servant to people who would betray Him and deny Him (Philippians 2:6-8). He felt the sting of this world and of death for people who didn't even love Him (John 15:18-25). Moreover, He willingly took on our sin to rescue believers from an eternity of death and separation from our Father (2 Corinthians 5:21). He came to bring you and me, the prodigal children, back to right standing with our Daddy, our Abba Father.

I can hardly believe someone would love me so much! In fact, sometimes it is so overwhelming to comprehend, that I would rather hang some Christmas garlands and go over my gift list than try to wrap my mind around the tremendous reality of Jesus pouring out His sacrificial love on the earth. Sometimes it is easier to brave the Christmas crowds at the mall than it is to *really* quiet my heart and ponder Him.

Perhaps the reason it is so difficult for us to grasp the gravity of what happened in that Bethlehem stable so long ago is because we do not truly understand God's immense love for us. We cannot fathom this amazing love that is unlike any we have ever known: a love that we do not have to strive to obtain (Ephesians 2:8-9), a love which comforts and heals (Psalm 147:3), is steadfast and unchanging (Psalm 86:15), and compels us to love one another (1 John 14:9).

What will it take for us to exchange a preoccupied heart of busyness for a heart of worship this Christmas? Let's pray, sister, that this year we will be able to understand more deeply than ever how wide and long and high and deep is God's great love for us (Ephesians 3:16-18), and pray that we will be able to rest in that love and finally find peace. This year, let us focus more on Jesus than on the "Christmas season."

Maybe we can sweep some of the Christmas craziness aside and *really, truly* focus on the love of our Savior. Do we really need all of these Christmas extras? Honestly, I probably don't. I need more time with my Savior, reading His Word—His love letter to me. That is what I want to spend time on this Christmas.

Years from now, it would be amazing to look back on this Christmas and be able to say "that was the year everything changed in my relationship with Jesus. That was the Christmas I truly started to follow Him." Maybe this is the Christmas we put our to-do lists aside and put everything we can into knowing Him deeper, into praying and fasting, asking the Holy Spirit to empower us to understand the immense love of Jesus. Will this be the Christmas that your heart is filled to overflowing with love for your Savior?

Indeed, every Christmas is one step closer to the year we spend Christmas with *our* Savior. Are you ready to meet Him? Let's get to know Him better this Christmas, delight in Him more, take our eyes off of what's going on around us and fix them on Him. Commit this Christmas to being the one in which you fall more deeply in love with Jesus. His gift to us is eternal, my friend, and better than anything under the tree this year!

Questions to Ponder

• Look deeply into your soul—do you *know* Jesus? If you were to meet Him face-to-face this very day, would you be ready? Would you like your walk with Him to be deeper? Would you like your love for Him to be stronger?

Faith-Filled Ideas

My friend, get on your knees and talk to God about these things. No matter where you are in your walk with the Lord, allow the Holy Spirit to do something new in your heart. Do not let this just be another Christmas. Let this be the year that everything changes. Make a commitment to walk more closely with Jesus, to rest deeper in Him, and to pray every day that you would have a greater love for Him than ever before. This is a Christmas you will want to remember!

_____

_____

_____

Journal

> For by grace you have been saved through faith.
> And this is not by your own doing; it is the gift of God,
> not a result of works, so that no one may boast.
>
> ~ Ephesians 2:8-9 (ESV)

"You can never truly enjoy Christmas until you can look up into the Father's face and tell Him you have received His Christmas gift."
~ John R. Rice

- Hello mamas! It's that sweet time of the day for you and Jesus to spend some one-on-one time. Grab a copy of the Word, a journal, and something yummy to drink, and truly lean into the Lord today. He has so much for you!

- Read Luke 2:8-20. I really want to encourage you to ponder and celebrate the true meaning of Christmas today. Rather than being overwhelmed and concerned about your checklists of things to do, dwell on blessings and be in awe of the ultimate gift of our Savior and Lord Jesus Christ.

The Wonder of Jesus

By: Sarah LaCroix

Wow! Is Christmas time already here again?

As I've become a young adult, I've started to notice that Christmas seems to have lost some of its dazzle and wonder. I now understand that flying reindeer don't exist, I've seen the Nutcracker a million times, and I actually ask for socks as a gift every year. The holidays get busy with parties and houses full of guests. My pockets get low on funds, and stress levels get high with the desire to fulfill wish lists.

When did wonder and the celebration of our Savior's birth shift to chaos and merely going through the motions?

Buried under all the Christmas checklists is a baby whose birth started this annual party, and I'm pretty sure he didn't ask for LEGO toys or Barbies. Mary never had Christmas trees or gingerbread houses for her kids. In fact, Jesus' childhood is barely mentioned in the Bible!

Don't get me wrong. I think Christmas traditions are absolutely fantastic, but maybe we are getting so consumed with all of the celebrations and festivities that we actually miss the beauty of the pure message of Christmas.

In the story of Jesus' birth, shepherds come, the heavenly hosts declare His birth, and powerful foreign men present our Savior with incredible wealth. And amidst the busyness, the Bible says, "But Mary treasured up all these things, and pondered them in her heart" (Luke 2:19).

She found value in the moments.

I believe Mary understood her baby was the Great I Am and that her obedience to God would reward her infinitely more than anything the world offered her.

Years later, when her baby would die on a cross, He was dying on her behalf. He died because of His tender love for all of people. He died to make a way for us to walk with His Father through life and join His Kingdom in our earthly passing. He died to pay for every mistake and every sin we've made so that we may take his hand and step over our painful pasts.

Mamas, Jesus wasn't born to give us stressful to-do lists: Jesus was born so we could celebrate life and have no fear for the future. I encourage you to ponder the gift and miracle of our Jesus' birth and to honor Him in your home this Christmas. Store up your moments, treasure your family, and be dazzled by the ultimate miracle.

Have a blessed and beautiful Christmas full of angels, cookies, and wonder.

Questions to Ponder

• Jesus has given you all His love and gifted you with His Spirit, sweet mama. It's so important to remember that! Take your time in celebrating that today. Talk to Him!

• How can you remind yourself and your family what this season is really about when you become stressed?

• What is your fondest Christmas memory or tradition? Ask yourself where you see God's hand in that memory, and be encouraged by that!

• Pray that God would fill you and your household with peace and graciousness this Christmas.

• Pray for a heart filled with joy and energy!

• Take the time to celebrate the wonder of Christmas, and try to see the season through the eyes of your kiddos. Everything is exhilarating, shiny, and wonderful!

Faith-Filled Ideas

Take some time today and work on making your heart obedient to recognizing the gift that Christmas offers you. Write out your list of Christmas miracles and joys. Keep this list somewhere easily accessible and pray praise over it.

As the classic Christmas carol states: "Rejoice! Rejoice! Emmanuel has come to thee, oh Israel (his people)!" Celebrate and encourage your heart with how God fulfills His promises for you and continues to bless you. It is so easy to get caught up with the things in life that are not going right, but I encourage your heart to *rejoice* in your numerous blessings!

journal

_____

_____

_____

_____

_____

_____

_____

journal

Journal

20 Days of Christmas Cheer

Help Club for Mom's *"Christmas Countdown!"*

20	19	18	17	16	15	14	13	12	11
10	9	8	7	6	5	4	3	2	1

We know it can be difficult to fill your Christmas season with FUN instead of constant busyness! So, at the Help Club for Moms, we have created the "20 Days of Christmas Cheer" countdown! Some ideas are purely for fun and others draw you closer to Jesus as a family! No need to complete them all, but it will surely be a Christmas to remember if you do!

DAY 20

Kids: Make a "Countdown to Christmas" paper chain out of red and green construction paper with 20 circles. Hang it somewhere for all to see in your home.

Moms: Look up these verses: Isaiah 7:14, John 1:14, Galatians 4:4-5, Isaiah 9:6, and 1 John 5:11. Choose your favorite one and work on memorizing it this Christmas season!

DAY 19

Kids: Read the story of Jesus' birth to your kids from Luke 2:1-21. Have your kids draw pictures of their favorite parts of the story. Then ask them to tell you about that aspect of the story as you write it on their illustration (or have them write it themselves). Staple all their pages together to make a Christmas book!

Moms: Take a bubble bath. While relaxing, prepare your heart and mind for a busy Christmas season. Pray that God would give you moments of rest and that you would soak in this season with your family.

DAY 18

Kids: Go to a bookstore and choose a special Christmas book to read together! Thrift stores are wonderful, too, for saving money. Most books are only 50 cents!

Moms: Plan an in-home date night for you and your husband. Surprise him with it and make sure you put it on your calendar so you don't forget.

DAY 17

Kids: Choose a Christmas hymn like *Away in the Manger, O Come All Ye Faithful,* or *Hark the Herald Angels Sing.* Sing it together often and try to learn all the words.

Moms: Text or call a friend or two and ask them if you can get coffee or tea together sometime soon. Taking time to connect with those you love is good for your heart!

20 Days
of Christmas Cheer

DAY 16

Kids: Make Christmas treats for your neighbors and deliver them. Rice Krispie treats are fast and easy!

Moms: Gather the family together and watch "The Nativity Story" together as a family!

DAY 15

Kids: Make or buy all the ingredients to make a Gingerbread House together. Frosting, graham crackers & sprinkles work wonderfully!

Moms: When the kids go to bed, choose one of your favorite Christmas movies and pop some popcorn. Let it be a treat to yourself!

DAY 14

Kids: Sip hot chocolate together as a family. Grab those mini-marshmallows kids love, sit at the table, and chat.

Moms: Make handmade gift tags as a family. They don't need to be perfect or fancy, just made with love!

DAY 13

Kids: Have your kids make a Christmas card to send to their Grandmas & Grandpas. No matter your child's age, their Grandparents will love them and keep them forever!

Moms: Think about a way you can bless your husband this Christmas. It could be anything: perhaps a little gift, an act of service for him, or making him his favorite meal.

DAY 12

Kids: Have a family picnic under the Christmas tree! Light a couple candles, turn off the lights, turn *up* the Christmas music, and make it *fun!*

Moms: Sit in the quiet. With kids, this is tough to do, but it can happen. Find small pockets of time to stop what you are doing and enjoy the quiet. If you make a habit of this, you will find yourself enjoying a few minutes of quiet each day.

DAY 11

Kids: Have your kids start thinking of a gift they can give to Jesus for Christmas. Maybe they can commit to treating others with kindness, talking to God more, etc. Set a special box under the tree for them to place their gifts written on pieces of paper.

Moms: Make a list! Our minds usually race with a million things during this holiday. Take about five minutes to write down all that is in your running to-do list in your mind. It will make you feel so much better when you are done!

20 Days
of
Christmas Cheer

DAY 10

Kids: Wrap your kids in toilet paper head to toe! Cut out carrots for their noses and black circles for their eyes! Watch them have fun and transform into *snowmen*, all at once!

Moms: Pray you will be flexible this season. We always have so many ideas and to-do's, but all of them simply cannot happen. Prepare your heart and mind for unmet expectations and interesting surprises.

DAY 9

Kids: Plan a "Candy Cane" hunt for your kids big and small! For the littles, make it easy around the house. For bigs, have them bundle up and search inside and outside. They can use paper bags to gather all the candy canes.

Moms: As you wrap presents this season, consider giving your kids "code names" so they can't guess their gifts. My mom would give us reindeer names but it would be fun to do names like "Candy Cane," "Gingerbread Man," "Snowball," etc.

DAY 8

Kids: Make a popcorn and cranberry garland to hang outside to feed the birds. The kids will love it!

Moms: Ask your husband or a friend to watch the kids one evening so you can wrap presents. Let this be a relaxing time for you. If gift bags make wrapping easier and more fun, do it! The wrapping doesn't need to be perfect.

DAY 7

Kids: Make Christmas ornaments together to add to the tree! It can be as simple as painting pine cones to elaborate Pinterest DIYs. Do what your family loves and don't make it too complicated.

Moms: Call a friend or family member to catch up. It can be for someone who really needs it, or maybe you really need it. God will show you who it is!

DAY 6

Kids: Have a "Snowball Toss!" Grab some clear or white plastic/styrofoam cups and draw snowmen faces on them. Put different points for each cup. Give your kids cotton balls and have them throw their "snowballs" into the cups for points. The player with the most points wins!

Moms: Plan what you will make for Christmas Eve & Christmas Day meals. Choose a mix of special and easy recipes. Go easy on yourself with a couple small special touches.

20 Days of Christmas Cheer

DAY 5

Kids: Go Christmas caroling around your neighborhood and spread some Christmas joy! Keep it simple or make it more fun with battery operated candles or hot cocoa in hand to enjoy as you sing.

Moms: Send a card to a friend or family member who could use some extra encouragement this season. Remind them of the love of Jesus!

DAY 4

Kids: Have a "shepherds dinner." Grab a loaf of bread at the grocery store and make a roast or stew. This would also be a great time to use a can of soup. Keep it simple. Lay a blanket on the floor and turn off all the lights (use flashlights for torches). Try to imagine what the shepherds felt as they witnessed the sky filled with angels singing praises to the newborn Savior.

Moms: While at the store, buy some flowers, or just one, to put in your home. Place it in a spot you will see it often. Sometimes it's the little things that change our attitude for the day!

DAY 3

Kids: Take the kids to go see your neighborhood Christmas lights. Driving around town to find the best ones is so much fun!

Moms: Turn on some Christmas music and do something you enjoy. Relax your heart before the busyness of the coming days.

DAY 2

Kids: Act out the nativity story! If desired, have your kids make props or simple costumes out of paper or cardboard; use whatever you have on hand. It doesn't have to be perfect, just have fun!

Moms: After your kids have gone to bed, turn off all the lights except the Christmas lights. Sit in the peace and quiet of the night and think about the beauty of your Savior and His great love for you.

DAY 1

Kids: Have a birthday party for Jesus! Make (or buy) a little cake or treat and celebrate our Savior together.

Moms: Make a list, on your own or as a family, of all the things you have to be thankful for this Christmas! God has blessed you in amazing ways!

Christmas
~ Week Two ~

Hello, My Friend!

Don't you just love this time of year? I don't know about you, but I have a tendency to take on more than I should at Christmas—more activities, more baking, more shopping, more fun! However, I am learning that more is not God's best for me or my family. The only thing my family really needs more of at this time of year is Jesus. I need to draw my children close and introduce them to our Savior in a deeper way. I need to show them what it looks like to bow my heart in worship before my King of Kings. I need to take a deep breath and encourage them to rest in His presence as the world rushes crazily around us.

Will you join me in this place of abiding peace? Will you choose to intentionally direct your children's hearts toward Jesus this season? Here are a few ideas for you this week as you teach your children how to stay close to the Lord this Christmas:

- Start each day off with a Christmas hymn. Sing together or simply just snuggle close and listen.
- Read a daily Christmas verse aloud to your children. There are some great lists of Christmas verses online.
- Stop and pray together. Try to find one aspect of our Lord's character to thank Him for each day.
- Help your children think of a gift to give Jesus this Christmas. Perhaps it is being kind toward someone in need of caring, showing the love of Christ to a person with whom they do not see eye-to-eye, or offering a heart of worship to the King of Kings! Pray together and ask God to open the right doors for you to serve others in love!

Remain in the love of Jesus with your children this Christmas, dear sister, and I promise it will be the most meaningful, soul-filling Christmas yet!

Peace and joy,
Tara Davis and the Help Club for Moms Team

> *But look for Christ and you will find Him,*
> *and with Him everything else thrown in.*
>
> ~ C.S. Lewis

Mom Tips

"I am the vine; you are the branches. If you remain in me and I in you, you will bear much fruit..." ~ John 15:5

The Wise Woman Builds Her Spirit

- Give yourself permission to indulge in your favorite treats. You know you're going to do it anyway, so enjoy it with moderation!
- Record Luke 2:9-14 on your phone recording device. Play this beautiful passage over and over this week to remind you of the beautiful night our Savior was born!

The Wise Woman Loves Her Husband

- Take time to prepare your husband's favorite meal this week. Have your children draw a menu for the evening.
- Find some ways to pamper your husband this month. Have a hot cup of cocoa ready when he gets home, set aside extra Christmas cookies just for him, write him a heartfelt Christmas card, or just remember to pause the Christmas preparations to give him a smile and a big kiss.

The Wise Woman Loves Her Children

- Purchase a toy with your children for "Angel Tree" or "Toys for Tots." Be sure to pray with your children for the child who will receive the gift. Pray for them to come to know Jesus at an early age and for Him to protect them and show them His love.
- Make December reading time extra special! Use wrapping paper to wrap up your favorite Christmas books (new, old, or from the library), and let your children unwrap them before you cuddle together to read the book. Wrap as many or as few as you want. You do you!

The Wise Woman Cares For Her Home

- Spend some time going through your children's toys getting rid of the ones they no longer play with, and making room for new ones. If the toys are in great condition and you have time, consider selling them on a trusted children's "buy and sell" Facebook page or find a ministry that gives gently used toys to foster or needy children.
- Make homemade Christmas potpourri to simmer on your stove. Use apples, oranges, cinnamon sticks, cloves, vanilla, even pine needles...use whatever you have on hand and fill your house with warmth and a delicious scent!

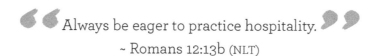

> **"** Always be eager to practice hospitality. **"**
> ~ Romans 12:13b (NLT)

"Hospitality means primarily the creation of free space where the stranger can enter and become a friend instead of an enemy. Hospitality is not to change people, but to offer them space where change can take place. It is not to bring men and women over to our side, but to offer freedom not disturbed by dividing lines."
~ Henri J.M. Nouwen

- Take a few minutes to call your prayer partner today. If you are having a hard time connecting to pray together, schedule a time and keep it short. If you're already in that habit, consider planning a longer phone call or a time to get together. Discuss prayers and praises.

- Find a quiet place to meet with God. Avoid distractions by keeping your area clear, turning your phone on airplane or night mode, and first praying that God will give you wisdom and speak to you through your study.

- Read James 2:14-26, writing verses 14-17 in your journal. Highlight or underline verse 17: "faith by itself, if it is not accompanied by action, is dead."

Love Thy Neighbor... with Parties & Tasty Treats

By: Heather Doolittle

I have a confession to make: I do not take rejection well. I avoid people who I expect will judge me, and when that's not possible, I keep them at arm's length. This is especially true when it comes to my faith in God; it impacts everything about me from the way I perceive the world to the way I raise my children to the way I spend my free time. I don't need everyone in my life to agree with me, but if someone looks down on me for my religion, they are insulting the very core of who I am. Hence, my sensitivity and self-centeredness have stood between me and the charge to "go into all the world" (Mark 16:15). I realize that I can't love or minister to people very well if I have built a wall between us, so I want to make an intentional effort to step out of my comfort zone and set aside my own feelings and fears of rejection.

In Matthew 16:18 (ESV), Jesus says, "...the gates of hell shall not prevail against [the church]." Gates are not an offensive weapon; the gates of Hell are a defense against the army of God. Satan is trying to keep us from realizing and sharing the peace, love, and salvation that are readily available to all. The gates of hell aim to separate the people who are led by the Spirit of God from those who need His Light, but Matthew 16:18 tells us that God will not allow this segregation to remain indefinitely. God's desire is for all of us to love and respect one another, even those who are lost or different, just as Jesus did. We as Christ-followers should reach out in love instead of feeding into Satan's plan by staying within our comfort zones and focusing inward.

You don't have to hold in-house Bible studies or become well-versed in apologetics to turn people to God. You can show people that God is love simply by inviting them into your imperfect life and loving them, putting your desire to know them above your desire to be perceived in a certain way. Be an example of how God calls us to love. Live differently by opening your heart and your home at a time when many people don't even know their neighbors and find it easier to do life alone.

The holiday season offers plenty of low-pressure opportunities to do this by inviting friends, distant family, and neighbors into our homes to get to know them and serve them with love. Christmastime is probably the one time of year when you can put up some Christ-centered décor, play Jesus-music, and invite over a group of believers and unbelievers alike without making anyone feel uncomfortable. Your agnostic neighbors may not be moved to tears by the sound of "Silent Night," but at least they're comfortable with the tune.

My dad used to say that life would be easy without the people! I can be a good neighbor: keep my lawn cut and dandelion-free, give out the good candy on Halloween, and remove my Christmas lights promptly on New Year's Day. However, God has a higher standard of "good," and it's entirely relational. Set aside the insignificant tasks and petty conflicts so you can focus on loving those around you. Satan wants to use your insecurities and fears to keep you stagnant, so resist that urge and step out of your comfort zone. If you only reach out to new friends when your house is spotless and you've made plenty of Christmas treats, you may never get to know them. Part of loving people in spite of their flaws is showing your own inadequacies and trusting them to accept you as you are.

Questions to Ponder

- Do the people around you know you're a Christian? If not, why? How can you live in a way that sets you apart?

- Consider your community (your neighborhood, your workplace, or your children's school, for example). How well do you really know those people? How can you make an effort to get to know them better?

- Is there anyone in that community who might need a friend? This person may be someone you tend to overlook. Ask God to show you who that person might be and how you can reach out to them. A simple card with a kind word or an invitation to Starbucks can be enough to start a new friendship or to brighten someone's life.

Faith-Filled Ideas

Plan a Christmas party for your kids' classmates, your neighbors, or some mom friends. Bonus for inviting new acquaintances or someone who is new to the neighborhood! Include at least a few people you wouldn't normally invite.

In theory, I love throwing parties, but when I'm in a busy season and don't have time to do something impressive, I'd rather just skip the extra work and tell myself I'll do it next year. I have to push myself to expand my horizons and make the added effort, and I consider it a service to God.

Don't put stress on yourself by trying to make everything perfect or by trying to make too much food. Just do what works best for you. Play Christmas hymns, serve simple treats, and just relax and get to know new friends.

If parties aren't your thing, pray and ask God how you can branch out and get to know your neighbors and others in your community. Deliver Christmas cookies with a smile and a sweet card, or deliver gift cards if baking isn't your forte. The point is to reach out and show hospitality and love, especially to those you wouldn't normally consider (they may be the ones who need it the most).

journal

> " I have come into the world as a light, so that no one who believes in me should stay in darkness. "
>
> ~ John 12:46

"The peace of God is not the absence of fear. It, in fact, is His presence."
~ Timothy Keller

- Take 10 minutes and reflect on your favorite Christmas song. Take in the beauty of the words and music, and write the words in your journal. To fully appreciate and understand the song, research the history of the author.

- Open your Bible and read the following verses about the birth of Jesus:
  - Matthew 1:18-23
  - Matthew 2:1-12
  - Luke 2:7
  - Luke 2:11-14
  - Revelation 12:1-5

What I learned from A Charlie Brown Christmas

By: Leslie Leonard

When I was in elementary school, one of the events I looked forward to most during Christmas was watching *A Charlie Brown Christmas* on television. I would look it up in our TV Guide and mark it on the calendar. We often watched it at school too. To me, it just did not feel like Christmas until I saw Charlie Brown decorate his little tree and Linus tell the story of what Christmas is all about. I loved Snoopy, Woodstock, and all the cast of Charlie Brown. My favorite Christmas gift as a young child was a stuffed Woodstock. In fact, I can clearly see a polaroid picture in my mind of my older brother and myself with my new toy that Christmas.

Linus is one of my favorite characters. I can really relate to him. He is uber responsible, fixes other people's problems, and often assesses the situation before acting. He is known for carrying around a security blanket. I myself carry around a "security blanket" everywhere I go too: a book, my phone, and a notebook. This way, I don't have to talk to people I don't know, and I always have something to do in awkward situations. These items help alleviate my fears of the unknown. I do not like the unknown. I feel very uncomfortable and uneasy. I choose to avoid the unknown. Are you like Linus too?

A few years ago, I was watching *A Charlie Brown Christmas* with my two girls, and I noticed something amazing. Linus is sharing what Christmas is all about, and he is quoting Scripture. He is specifically quoting Luke 2:8-14 (ESV) which states:

> And in the same region there were shepherds out in the field, keeping watch over their flock by night. And an angel of the Lord appeared to them, and the glory of the Lord shone around them, and they were filled with great fear. And the angel said to them, "Fear not, for behold, I bring you good news of great joy that will be for all the people. For unto you is born this day in the city of David a Savior, who is Christ

the Lord. And this will be a sign for you: you will find a baby wrapped in swaddling cloths and lying in a manger." And suddenly there was with the angel a multitude of the heavenly host praising God and saying, "Glory to God in the highest, and on earth peace among those with whom he is pleased!"

Here is the amazing part: Linus drops the blanket right at the moment he states "Fear not." He stands alone on stage without that blanket and finishes the verses. When he is done speaking, he calmly picks up his blanket. What I learned from this is that the birth of Jesus separates us from our fears. We can fully trust in Jesus Christ and lean into Him.

Here is a list of blanket truths that I learned from *A Charlie Brown Christmas*:

- The birth of Jesus brought Him close to us (Matthew 1:21).
- The birth of Jesus has removed the fear of the unknown (Philippians 4:6-7).
- The birth of Jesus frees us from the habits that we are unable to break ourselves (1 Corinthians 10:13).
- The birth of Jesus has removed the fear of being alone (John 3:16).
- The birth of Jesus simply lets us trust in Him instead of grasping false security (John 15:16).
- Jesus is accessible to all (Ephesians 2:18).

For many of us, the simplest truths of the Gospel bring the most encouragement. May you find peace and hope this Christmas in knowing your Savior loves you and is the source of all you need.

Questions to Ponder

- Do you live a life of fear? I hope not! It has been said that there are 365 "Fear Nots" in the Bible. One for every day of the year. Psalm 56:3-4 states "When I am afraid, I will trust in you. In God, whose word I praise, in God I trust; I will not be afraid. What can mortal man do to me?"

- My charge to you is to trust God more this next year, set aside your fears, and live a life of joy. Journal about your top 5 fears and turn them over to God. Revisit this entry every three months to note your progress. Are you still fearful? Have you fully given that fear over to God? I hope so!

Faith-Filled Ideas

Watch *A Charlie Brown Christmas* with your family one night this week. Pop some popcorn, make some hot chocolate, and snuggle on the couch. Pay special attention to Linus's speech. After the movie, pull out your family Bible and read Luke 2:8-14 as a family. Answer any questions your children might have. Bonus tip: have your children act out the scene while you read the Bible.

Journal

_____

_____

_____

_____

_____

Journal

Christmas

> **"** For God so loved the world that he gave his one and only Son, that whoever believes in him shall not perish but have eternal life. **"**
>
> ~ John 3:16

"All the Christmas presents in the world are worth nothing without the presence of Christ."
~ David Jeremiah

- Grab your Bible, journal, and hot drink. Now is your time to breathe and be alone with God!

The Season of Giving

By: Samantha Swanson

One of my favorite family traditions is so simple, yet so fun: Secret Santa.

Each year (on Thanksgiving if we're thinking ahead, otherwise early December!), my family gathers together and draws names for a gift exchange.

Honestly, half the fun in this tradition is learning how to successfully keep your assigned name a secret. In my family, my brother and especially my dad will attempt to trick the girls—my sister and I—into revealing the names we drew. I confess I've accidentally let my name slip before, and I am reminded of this often. It's a good thing I've been taught to be able to laugh at myself!

Anyway, here's how Secret Santa works: Once we draw the names and before anyone goes shopping, we decide how much each person is allowed to spend on their Secret Santa gift. We didn't want Dad going all out while my 7-year-old sister found that her budget was only large enough for a couple packs of gum.

When we were younger, the max amount each person could spend was $10, but we've pushed it up to $20 now that we're older. Believe it or not, the limit makes it more fun! Secret Santa is not about purchasing the most expensive or extravagant gift. It's about getting creative, resourceful, and thoughtful—thinking about something meaningful that will make one person in our family smile.

The next step is choosing what time we will open our Secret Santa gifts. In our house, while the other gifts waited until Christmas Day, we have designated Christmas Eve as our time for this particular gift exchange.

This tradition is so easy and gets everyone involved. It's something each of us looks forward to year after year.

It turns out, though, my parents weren't just fun, they were clever because Secret Santa taught me from a young age that Christmas is about more than "toys, toys, toys."

Maybe it does feel like Christmas has become all about the presents under the tree.

The good news? Secret Santa is different. This tradition taught my siblings and me to give rather than simply receive.

Looking back, I can see that sometimes we bought presents with ourselves in mind, not necessarily thinking about the person who would be receiving the gift. One year, my little brother presented me a bear-shaped slingshot after spending a good 20 minutes "testing" it out in the backyard. That memory still gives us a good laugh!

As we've grown, things have changed. We've learned to buy or create gifts with the other person in mind. Sometimes the gift is funny, and sometimes it's sweet, but either way, we have learned the joy of presenting to a person we love something they will want, need, or enjoy.

And it turns out that teaching your children the beauty of giving is the perfect time to share with them the most precious gift they will ever receive: the gift of Christ.

"For God so loved the world that he gave his one and only Son, that whoever believes in him shall not perish but have eternal life" (John 3:16).

Questions to Ponder

• How are you going to teach your children about the joy of giving this Christmas?

• Have you ever taken the time to tell your children the reason why we give gifts on this holiday? Talk about the Wise Men's gifts to Jesus and the gift of eternal life that God has promised to us through his Son. If you haven't ever thought about why we give gifts, or just don't know a great answer to this question, look it up and share what you find with your kids. There are so many helpful and explanatory sites online!

Faith-Filled Ideas

If you want to try Secret Santa but your children are young and don't have much money, you could try one of two things. One idea is to find special jobs around the house to earn a few dollars to spend on a gift. Or, encourage them to create a gift for their Secret Santa recipient: write and illustrate a short picture book, sew a small pillow (I did this a lot when I was little!), write a poem or draw or paint something their gift recipient will love. There are so many ways to get creative!

Journal

_____

_____

_____

_____

_____

_____

_____

_____

_____

_____

journal

Christmas ~ Week Two ~ Day Six

Christmas morning is such a joyous time of gift gifting, paper ripping, and squeals from pleased children. At our house, all five kids know to wait until mom and dad have a cup of coffee before anyone can open gifts. I have learned from years of experience that I don't want to be in the kitchen all day long, so prepping our breakfast the night before is a welcome reward for a bit of intentionality. The streusel and syrup in this recipe can also be made the night before; so while coffee is brewing, all I need to do is preheat the oven for a Christmas morning Cinnamon Bread Pudding Breakfast. Bread Pudding is similar to French toast but has more of a cake-like, spongy texture. I will tell you that we have made the typical cinnamon roll French Toast casseroles where you just open the cinnamon roll cans, bake, and smother with cream cheese icing. Although they are easy to make, we have found that they lack unique homemade flavor. This recipe uses Cinnabon™ creamer, real cream cheese, and maple syrup, and has been voted the winning breakfast casserole in our family! We look forward to this frosted goodness every Christmas morn!

CINNAMON OVERNIGHT BREAD PUDDING WITH CREAM CHEESE SYRUP

By: Rae-Ellen Sanders

Ingredients:

A loaf of French Bread

6 Eggs

1 ½ cups of Cinnabon™ flavored creamer

½ cup brown sugar

1 tablespoon Vanilla Extract

Streusel Topping:

½ cup all-purpose flour

½ cup firmly packed brown sugar

1 teaspoon cinnamon

¼ teaspoon salt

8 tablespoons cold butter, cut into pieces

Cream Cheese Syrup:

4 ounces of cream cheese (half of a brick)

¼ cup (4 tablespoons) butter

¼ cup maple syrup

1 teaspoon vanilla extract

1 cup confectioners sugar

¼ cup of milk

Directions:

1. Grease a 9x13-inch baking pan. Cut bread into cubes and spread evenly in the pan.

2. In a medium-sized bowl, mix together eggs, creamer, brown sugar, and vanilla.

3. Pour evenly over the bread. Cover tightly and store in the refrigerator overnight.

TO MAKE STREUSEL:

1. Mix flour, brown sugar, cinnamon, and salt. Add butter pieces and cut them into the dry mixture until crumbly (food processor is the preferred method). Store in a zipper bag in the fridge.

2. Preheat oven to 350 degrees. Remove casserole from the refrigerator and sprinkle crumb mixture over the top.

3. Bake for 1 hour, uncovered.

FOR SYRUP:

1. Beat cream cheese, butter, maple syrup, and vanilla at medium speed with an electric mixer.

2. Gradually incorporate powdered sugar.

3. Add milk and beat until smooth.

4. Heat up in the microwave before pouring over your Cinnamon Overnight Bread Pudding, or serve on the side. This treat is sweet enough without the syrup but absolutely heavenly with it.

~Christmas~
~ Week Three ~

Hello, Dearest Mama,

Well, can you believe it's almost Christmas?! How are you doing, sweet friend? Are you feeling stressed by all the preparations and demands on your time? Is the thought of traveling or hosting family beginning to cause you anxiety?

Do you feel hopeful this wonderful Christmas season or just plain stressed out?

Why does Christmas, the season where we celebrate the birth of our loving Savior, make us crabby and grouchy? Why do we seem to get annoyed with family members at a time when we should be showing them the most love? Why do we easily engage in conflict over our wants and desires?

Perhaps the answer lies in adjusting our expectations and dreams of how we want our Christmas to look and feel. After all, it is Jesus' birthday, not ours! When we think of celebrating Christmas in the light of the desires of Jesus' heart for His children, it changes everything! We begin to shift the focus away from ourselves and onto Christ and surrender our will to His. This one change in our thinking can revolutionize this time of year for our families and deepen our relationships with the Lord and with others.

How would Jesus want us to celebrate His birthday? That is a great question to ask.

This week, take a moment and ask Jesus to show you how He would want you to walk with Him through this Christmas season. Ask Him to help you to see your circumstances and the people in your life from His perspective. Seek His help to love others as He does. He will help you, and, who knows, maybe this will be your best Christmas ever!

Merry Christmas!

Love,
Deb Weakly and Help Club for Moms Team

Loving people is the highest level of spiritual warfare that we could ever do.

~ Joyce Meyer

Mom Tips

"I am the vine; you are the branches. If you remain in me and I in you, you will bear much fruit..." ~ John 15:5

The Wise Woman Builds Her Spirit

- This Christmas season, feel free to slow down and say "no." Don't let the busyness of the season cause you stress. Say "no" so you can say "yes" to rest.

- Take time for yourself. You can't fill from an empty cup! Be sure to dig into God's Word this week! He wants to fill you with His Holy Spirit and shower you with His love.

The Wise Woman Loves Her Husband

- Ask your husband what his favorite Christmas treat or tradition is and make that a priority to do with him or for him.

- Plan something special that your husband will enjoy this week! Whether it is a night out or in together, doing a fun activity, or even just giving him some time alone to decompress from the busyness of the Christmas season, you know your husband best!

The Wise Woman Loves Her Children

- Take time this week to read your children the Christmas story directly from God's Word, Luke 2:1-20.

- Have a snowflake making contest. Even little ones can make simple snowflakes! See who can cut out the most detailed snowflake, the silliest, the most creative, the largest, the smallest, etc. Use the snowflakes to decorate windows in your home!

The Wise Woman Cares For Her Home

- Set a timer for 20 minutes, play some fun Christmas music, and clean up your house for Christmas. It is easier to enjoy your family and focus on Jesus when we are not distracted by clutter and mess.

- Sometimes it's difficult to be content with our home when it's not perfectly decorated or "House Beautiful." But to our children, the most important decoration in our home is our love. Don't strive for a perfect home if it causes you stress and makes you grouchy. Let your home be a living laboratory of life, not perfection. Focus on creating memories of fun and laughter this coming year instead of stress!

> The Lord your God is in your midst, a mighty one who will save;
> he will rejoice over you with gladness; he will quiet you by his love.
>
> ~ Zephaniah 3:17 (ESV)

Christmas

"God loves each of us as if there were only one of us."
~ St. Augustine

- Remember to call your prayer partner today. In the midst of the holiday season, it is so important to keep praying with one another. Now is a time when most of us need extra prayer to get through the stress and busyness, so don't give up!

- Before you start your study today, calm your heart to hear from God. Psalm 46:10 reminds us to stop and be still. Sit down with your Bible, journal, and a pen. Ask God to speak to you during this time, and then write down what He says to you.

- Make a reminder on your calendar to call your prayer partner this week. It is so encouraging to pray with one another!

A Note from Your Father to You this Christmas

By: Kristi Valentine

As we count down to Christmas, I strongly sense God saying, "Tell moms that I love them." How beautiful! The unfathomable God who formed the universe is also your loving Father and wants you to know how much He cherishes you.

All over the Bible, His love can be found. In Ephesians, it's described as a more deep and profound love than can be understood. Zephaniah 3:17 says that God rejoices over us with gladness. James 1:17 shares that every good and perfect gift in our lives is from our Heavenly Father. Oh, that is so good!

How do we respond to God's love, especially during the busyness of Christmas? How will you respond to the One who is rejoicing over you right now? Rejoicing! Who loves like that? Only Him.

In the gospels, Jesus unveiled that the most important thing to do is love the Lord with all our heart, soul, mind, and strength. What does it look like to love God like that? When was the last time you did that? Consistently loving Him with our all is a right response to One who adores us with a love so joyful, glad, good, and perfect! In Luke 10:38-42 (NLT), Mary of Bethany painted a gorgeous glimpse of the response that pleased Jesus:

> As Jesus and the disciples continued on their way to Jerusalem, they came to a certain village where a woman named Martha welcomed them into her home. Her sister, Mary, sat at the Lord's feet, listening to what He taught. But Martha was distracted by the big dinner she was preparing. She came to Jesus and said, "Lord, doesn't it seem unfair to you that my sister just sits here while I do all the

work? Tell her to come and help me." But the Lord said to her, "My dear Martha, you are worried and upset over all these details! There is only one thing worth being concerned about. Mary has discovered it, and it will not be taken away from her."

Jesus' words, "There is only one thing worth being concerned about," deeply provoke my heart. God reveals what He's longing for from us! His love for us is immeasurable and poured out, and, in return, He's looking for a Mary of Bethany, one who prioritizes worshipping and abiding in Him.

In light of this, with all the Christmas decorating, shopping, cooking, and cleaning, how will you make time to abide in Him? What can you take off your plate, release to God this season, and not take back? Is it strained relationships, stressful finances, or something else?

In Jeremiah 29:13, God promises, "You will find me, when you seek me with all your heart." Abide in Him, and He will show you how much He loves you. Right now, He is inviting you in, to surrender your heart, so He can open your eyes and show you His glory.

So I pray, "God, as you proclaim Your word over your daughters, open our eyes to your love for us. Teach us how to abide and do the *one thing* worth being concerned about, as Jesus told Martha. Whisper to us now how to sit at your feet, even with a wealth of tasks at hand this Christmas."

Questions to Ponder

- Take a moment to contemplate what your heart really longs for. Is it sitting at the feet of Jesus and listening to what He wants to say to you? Or something else? Be honest. He already knows anyway! Ask Him for help to love Him in a way that pleases Him.

- If you fully believed that God loves you the way the Bible describes, how would you live your life differently?

Faith-Filled Ideas

This Christmas, read the story of Mary of Bethany from Luke 10:38-42 with your children. Let them soak in the idea that Jesus is more concerned with our hearts loving, seeking, and abiding in Him than anything else in life. Then brainstorm with your children about how your family can carve out more time to do that. Maybe it means not having things as perfect as you'd like this Christmas. Perhaps your family will have to say "no" to something. Either way, rejoice in knowing that your family has pleased God by abiding in Him and focusing on the "one thing worth being concerned about."

Journal

_____

_____

_____

_____

_____

_____

journal

> **" "** But Mary kept all these things like a secret treasure in her heart.
> She thought about them over and over. **, ,**
>
> ~ Luke 2:19 (NIrV)

"So God throws open the door of this world—and enters as a baby. As the most vulnerable imaginable. Because He wants unimaginable intimacy with you. What religion ever had a god that wanted such intimacy with us that He came with such vulnerability to us? What God ever came so tender we could touch Him? So fragile that we could break Him? So vulnerable that His bare, beating heart could be hurt? Only the One who loves you to death."
~ Ann Voskamp

- Get a warm drink, find a comfortable spot, and enjoy a few moments with God!

- Read Luke 1:26-56, Luke 2:4-7 and Luke 2:19, Deuteronomy 6:1-9

Mary, the Mother of Jesus

By: Kathryn Egly

I have four young boys, so there have been four Christmas nights that I've been awake through the quiet hours of the night and early morning with a newborn. These moments always give me a chance to reflect on the very first Christmas.

What was Mary thinking and feeling as she held her little one in her arms in those quiet moments? Was she scared? Excited? Curious? Joyful? Luke 2:19 tells us "But Mary treasured up all of these things and pondered them in her heart." What was she pondering?

I stare into my little boy's face and wonder: Who will he become? Did Mary know who Jesus would become?

Was she overwhelmed at the thought that God had entrusted her to raise His Son—a child who would bring Hope and Peace for all eternity? Was she afraid she might do something wrong?

As I hold my little ones in my arms, I too, can begin to feel afraid. Though I didn't give birth to Jesus, I am raising a child of God! A child who has the potential to bring hope to a hurting world. A child who can bring the Good News to others! What if I mess up? Do I have what it takes? Then I remember that God chose this child for me at this time.

Deuteronomy 31:6 tells us, "Be strong and courageous. Do not be afraid or terrified...for the Lord your God goes with you; he will never leave you nor forsake you."

Wow, just bask in those words for a minute. We don't need to fear. Our Father God never leaves us. He is with us!

What are things we, as mothers, can do to mold these young lives as they become followers of Christ and make a positive difference in this world?

Most importantly, ask for God's help every single day! Ask Him for wisdom because James 1:5 tells us "If any of you lacks wisdom, you should ask God, who gives generously to all without finding fault, and it will be given to you."

God will give you the wisdom and strength to be the best mother you can be. Rely on *Him!* Allow Him to empower you every minute of every day!

Here are some other suggestions for raising young men and women of God:

- First, stay present. Look at your children in the eye and answer their questions.
- Smile and remind them that they are loved—by you and by God!
- Say "I'm sorry" when you mess up. (We all mess up!)
- Talk about the goodness of God—sharing stories of what He has done in your life and the lives of others. Deuteronomy 6:7 instructs us to "Talk about them when you sit at home and when you walk along the road, when you lie down and when you get up."
- Pray together—for their "owies," for their friends, and for their concerns.
- Sing and read together.
- Love their Daddy. (If you are separated or divorced, continue to speak only good things about their dad).

Above all—rely on God and ask for His divine help.

Each day is a new day: an opportunity to ask God for help; a new day to stay present in your children's lives; a chance to watch for what God is already doing in your child's heart and life; and an occasion to come alongside to encourage that work!

God chose you for this task and with His help, you can do the incredible work of raising a child of God!

Questions to Ponder

- Ask God to show you how to be the best mother you can be. (Write down what He puts on your heart.)
- How can I invest in myself?
- How can I intentionally invest in my children in the coming year?

Faith-Filled Ideas

Talk with your children about the good things God has done in your life!

Tell your children what you love about God.

Ask them what they love about their Heavenly Father.

_____

_____

_____

Journal

Christmas

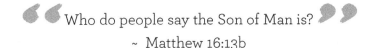

> **" "** Who do people say the Son of Man is? **" "**
> ~ Matthew 16:13b

Christmas

"The vision of Christ that thou dost see
Is my vision's greatest enemy:
Thine has a great hook nose like thine,
Mine has a snub nose like to mine...
Both read the Bible day and night,
But thou read'st black where I read white."
~ William Blake

- Have a seat in a quiet place, perhaps with some hot cocoa, and think about the man you are celebrating this Christmas season. Who is He to you? How would you describe Him?

- Read Micah 5:2 and Isaiah 7:14, prophecies of Jesus' birth.

More Than We Know: This Is Jesus

By: Elise Turner

The more I learn about Jesus, the more I fall in love with Him. I'm happy to know that He is not just the man I learned about in Sunday school, always with a gentle smile on His face and painted among children, rainbows, and baby sheep. Jesus challenges our conceptions of deities and authority figures. He is more than we know and better than we know. Like a constantly evolving partner, He is perfect for us in every season. The Gospels only tell half the story of who Jesus was and is. Scriptures before and after—from the Old Testament to Revelation—allude to His revolutionary impact. This Christmas, celebrate Jesus the baby, born in perfect peace to a modest woman and her husband. But appreciate, also, the complex character of a man who is like no other.

These are just a few reasons to celebrate our Savior:

- **Jesus is closer than we think.**
  When Jesus died on the cross, He enabled unlimited access to His presence. Because His presence is not only with us but also within us, we can never escape Him. He moves with us. He feels with us, and He has experienced the whole human spectrum of emotion, so His empathy is unrivaled. Jesus is more sophisticated than any other god, who controls beings from on high, bringing unexplainable disaster and performing sporadic miracles at the snap of a finger. He's not just watching us from His throne; He's with us in our homes, getting his hands dirty with our family problems and messy emotions, because He cares. That's why He gave up His position of glory and came down to the dirt: to bring us up from the dirt, into healing and redemption. Because of Jesus, we never have to approach God in fear. We never have to wonder if He hears us or if He cares. He is always closer than we think.

- **Jesus is peace.**
  If you are feeling anxiety or unrest, that is not from Jesus. Jesus came so that we would have peace in our world and individually. Philippians 4:6-7 (NLT) tells us, "Do not worry about anything; instead, pray about everything. Tell God what you need, and thank him for all he has done. Then you will experience God's peace, which exceeds anything we can understand. His peace will guard your hearts and minds as you live in Christ Jesus." These verses are a promise to us—that as Jesus is in us, we are guaranteed peace of mind and heart. So, if our minds are focused on the man nearest to us and not on our fleshly concerns, they will be free.

- **Jesus is approachable.**
  We may read the Old Testament and think that God is harsh and unapproachable. I am guilty of seeing Him as far-off and comfortably seated on His throne of judgment. I know that when I sin, I'm scared to face Him. I think He doesn't want to hear from me, that I'm better off trying again in a couple of days when the sin has "worn off." This mindset completely disregards God's decision to send Jesus to the earth so we can access Him more easily. He chose to send a man of flesh and blood, whom we could relate to, and He sent Him first as a harmless baby of humble birth. We are all familiar with the presence that babies bring to our families—they are inviting, unifying, and effortlessly loving. Jesus is as easily loved and loving as a baby. He is not threatening. God orchestrated every detail of Jesus' birth to foreshadow who He would be to us, a God who we can approach boldly and frequently.

Take time this Christmas to think about the life of our Savior—His birth, death, and everything in between—and how that makes Him, unlike any other man or god, meet and exceed all expectations we may have for Him.

Questions to Ponder
• How have you limited Jesus in the way you think about Him? Are you guilty of seeing Him as distant and impersonal, as a mere figure in a story?

Faith-Filled Ideas
When you read the Gospels, pay close attention to Jesus: notice what He says and does, and ask the Holy Spirit to show you more and more about Him.

If you are looking for reading material on the character of Jesus, check out *The Jesus I Never Knew* by Philip Yancey.

journal

_____

_____

_____

_____

_____

_____

journal

Food for the Soul

The Christmas holidays are filled with family, friends, fun celebrations and *lots* of food! If you are like me, this is the time of year where you find sickness lurking around every corner, waiting to attack in response to the excess stress and the rich foods you've been eating.

Why not try something new this year? Feed your body what it yearns for: spinach, fruit and healthy nutrients! After all, a smoothie a day helps keep the doctor away!

DELICIOUS AND NUTRITIOUS HOLIDAY GREEN SMOOTHIE

By: Deb Weakly

Ingredients:

2 cups spinach (I freeze mine. Not only does it stay fresh much longer, but it takes the place of ice in the smoothie)
1 cup frozen blueberries
1 cup frozen strawberries
1 banana
1 portion of a powdered fruit and vegetable supplement. I use "Life Greens" from Lifetime Fitness (Mixed Berry). It is absolutely delicious and adds lots of antioxidants.
Enough water to cover the top of the smoothie mixture

   Note: I use all organic ingredients purchased at Costco.

Directions:

1. Mix in blender or Magic Bullet until really smooth and there are no chunks of spinach.

2. This mixture is for a large sized container for a Magic Bullet. If you have a medium container, go ahead and split the recipe in half. This makes 2 servings. My hubby and I both love our green smoothies in the morning!

   Enjoy!

Christmas
~ Week Four ~

Merry Christmas, Friend!

One of my favorite songs at this time of year is *A Strange Way to Save the World* by 4Him. It makes me cry every time I hear the beautiful lyrics floating across the radio waves;

> I'm sure he must have been surprised at where this road had taken him 'cause never in a million lives would he have dreamed of Bethlehem. And standing at the manger, he saw with his own eyes the message from the angel come to life. And Joseph said, "Why me? I'm just a simple man of trade. Why Him, with all the rulers in the world? Why here, inside this stable filled with hay? Why her? She's just an ordinary girl. Now, I'm not one to second guess what angels have to say, but this is such a strange way to save the world..."

The humble circumstances in which God chose to send His Son into this dark and broken world never ceases to amaze me. God could have chosen anyone—a beautiful queen like Esther or a mighty king like David—and yet, He chose a poor carpenter and a young girl as His vessel to carry and bear the Savior of the World. The witnesses to this birth were not men of means or influence but the lowest of the low; ragged shepherds.

You see, God uses ordinary means and people to do extraordinary things. Jesus, born in a stable rather than a palace as He deserved, was made accessible to everyone. As Luke 2:10 reminds us, "But the angel said to them, 'Do not be afraid. I bring you good news that will cause great joy for *all* the people.'" That includes you and me, as well as the grimy beggar on the street corner or the pop stars that cover the tabloids in the supermarket. Jesus came to redeem and restore *all* people.

So, as you're wrapping gifts and enjoying Christmas festivities with your family and friends, do as Jesus' mother Mary did—ponder these things in your heart. Thank God for sending His Son to redeem mankind. Pray for Him to show you the "lowest of the low" this Christmas season; those who desperately need to know the love of Jesus, the ones we often forget in our own "busy." Perhaps He will lead you to make a donation to the local homeless ministry or buy a warm meal for someone on the street corner. Maybe He will prompt you to pray for the airbrushed beauty pictured in the newsstand in front of you or invite a lonely neighbor over for Christmas dinner. Remember, God uses ordinary means and people to do extraordinary things. Be *extraordinary* to someone this Christmas and embrace *this strange way to save the world!*

Love & Blessings,
Rebekah Measmer and the Help Club for Moms Team

But Mary treasured up all these things and pondered them in her heart.

~ Luke 2:19

Mom Tips

"I am the vine; you are the branches. If you remain in me and I in you, you will bear much fruit..." ~ John 15:5

The Wise Woman Builds Her Spirit

- Take some time to think of something you want to give Jesus this year. Maybe you have been holding back from giving Him every part of your heart, maybe you want to spend more time with Him in prayer or in His Word, perhaps you want to fall more deeply in love with Him than ever before. Don't commit this gift to Jesus with your words only, make a plan to implement it throughout the coming year.

- Read the story of Christ's birth in Luke 1-2. Think of how Mary must have felt as Jesus' mother. Praise God for the absolute blessing He has given you in allowing you to be a mother to His precious little ones!

The Wise Woman Loves Her Husband

- How can you bless your husband during this busy week? Take some time to serve him in a way that is meaningful to him!

- Pray that your husband will know the depth of the Savior's love for him! Pray that he will seek Jesus in a new, deeper way this Christmas.

The Wise Woman Loves Her Children

- Choose to show your children the love of their Savior in an even greater way this week! The week of Christmas can be stressful, with many events, preparation, baking, cleaning, or traveling. When you feel frustrated, don't speak, pray! God will give you a peaceful spirit and words of gentleness for your family!

- Act out the story of Jesus' birth this week with your children! You don't need fancy costumes or a script. Read the story from either a children's Bible or the first part of Luke, and let your kids take control of the props and acting! This type of playtime will make the true meaning of Christmas even more real to your children! You can even do this with older kids! It will likely turn out much more humorous, but what a meaningful family tradition to start!

The Wise Woman Cares For Her Home

- Try to have short, 15-minute family clean up times daily throughout this week. Your house will stay relatively clean, and you will be able to enjoy some rest during this Christmas week!

- Take some time to really sit and soak up all the ways, large and small, God has provided for you and blessed you this past year, the greatest of which is the gift of Jesus!

> **"** But one thing I do: Forgetting what is behind and straining toward what is ahead, I press on toward the goal to win the prize for which God has called me heavenward in Christ Jesus. **"**
>
> ~ Philippians 3:13b-14

"And what happened then? Well, in Whoville they say that the Grinch's small heart grew three sizes that day. And then the true meaning of Christmas came through, and the Grinch found the strength of ten Grinches plus two."
~ Dr. Seuss

- Remember to call your prayer partner today. Pray over your Christmas celebrations, your guests, the work you have left to do, and whatever else comes to mind.

- It's time to meet with Jesus! He is the One who gave all He had so you can have the great hope of a rich life. Grab your Bible, journal, a candle, and something hot and delicious to drink and go to the place where you meet with your Savior.

- Read Philippians 3:13b-14, Psalm 9:1b, and 1 Thessalonians 5:16-18 slowly and out loud. Write these powerful verses in your journal. Pray and ask the Holy Spirit to speak to your heart today.

The Memories Are All That's Left

By: Deb Weakly

I'm sad to say it, but last Christmas season, my husband and I had way too much "Grinch" (our hearts were three sizes too small), and way too little of the "good tidings of great joy" that is supposed to come during the Christmas season. We were simply stressed out and super tired, which we all know is a recipe for discord in any marriage. Preparing for Christmas is a lot of work, especially for the woman of the house, and I felt disappointed and sad.

The good news is that when I awoke on December 27th, God began a work in my heart. I repented and asked God to help me remember the good times and not dwell on anything that recently went wrong. My hubby and I talked about our bad attitudes and told each other we were sorry. We then started naming the blessings God had given us and all the ways He had answered our prayers. We finished our time together with a moment of prayer, thanking God for His goodness and our fun memories. The words of Psalm 9:1 came alive in our hearts.

> I will give thanks to the Lord with my whole heart; I will recount all of your wonderful deeds. (Psalm 9:1 ESV)

Yes, God has been good to us. Through thankfulness and focusing on the good, our hearts began to feel lighter as we reframed our memories from that Christmas. Now when I look back, I remember the sweet moments of our family playing games, laughing, and enjoying one another's company, and celebrating the birth of Jesus together.

Reframing a memory with the help of the Holy Spirit is one practical way we can "Be joyful always, pray at all times, be thankful in all circumstances" (1 Thessalonians 5:16-18a GNT). Reframing doesn't say the event never happened, it just causes us to notice the goodness of God, no matter what we've been through.

I have heard that the process of reframing is similar to changing a picture in a picture frame. The frame is still the same, but the picture within the frame is different. Simply put, your situation hasn't changed, but the way you look at that situation is different. When we change our view of a painful situation, it helps to heal our hearts, which leads to a more joy-filled and content life. Life will never be perfect; it will always be a mixture of good and bad.

One last thing: it's important to remember we have an enemy who hates Christian families and will do whatever he can to cause division in yours. He will try to get you to harbor bitterness and unforgiveness in your heart against someone you love and wants your memories of time with family, especially at Christmas, to be tainted with thoughts of disappointment and feeling offended from something someone said to you. Ask God to help you reframe any memories you may have and to forgive. Pray with a friend and then ask for accountability any time you start to complain or gripe about someone or something that happened.

What will you choose to remember about this Christmas?

Questions to Ponder

• Before Christmas week begins, write the answers to these questions in your journal:

1. What has been fun about your Christmas season so far?

2. Visualize your Christmas. How would you like it to go? Since you can only change your attitude and not anyone else's, write down how you want to act. For example: "This Christmas, I will prayerfully be kind and patient. I will laugh a lot and be fun to be around. With God's help, I can do this!" Review this several times before the big day arrives!

• After Christmas is over, write the answer to these questions in your journal too:

1. What was challenging about this Christmas? Do I need to seek forgiveness from anyone?

2. Who could use an encouraging "thank you" from me? Send this ASAP!

3. What are my top 3-5 fun memories from this year? Ask your kids this same question. Read these aloud once each day until January 2nd. This will help you and your family to reframe your memories and begin storing up many decades of a beautiful life in your heart and mind. Pray a little prayer of thanksgiving for the sweet memories of your Christmas this year.

Faith-Filled Ideas

Remember what I call, "The Danger of the Last Day." Just like Satan came to tempt Jesus *after* He was hungry, he will tempt you and your family to get angry or bitter when you are at your lowest and most tired. If you have been traveling, you and your family are out of routine and the kids can be grouchy. A family member may choose to be critical of your tired wee ones, and you may become offended, which can taint even the most festive of Christmas celebrations. Pray this simple prayer, "Come, Holy Spirit," several times during the day if you have to, and ask the Lord for extra grace to be kind and sweet to your family.

If you are hosting, you might be like I was this Christmas - so tired I could hardly make it until 9:30 at night. I was very vulnerable to tears this Christmas simply because I was tired. Give yourself the rest you need. Take a nap, or maybe go for a brisk walk to get your blood pumping.

Even though it's Christmas and we have lots of treats around the house to tempt us, try a green smoothie with plenty of spinach but also delicious blueberries, bananas, and strawberries, and some sort of nutritional boost. Take care of yourself, mama. If you don't, who will?

journal

Journal

Christmas

You will keep in perfect peace those whose minds are steadfast,
because they trust in you. Trust in the LORD forever,
for the LORD, the LORD, is the Rock eternal.

~ Isaiah 26:3

"Our experience of communion can fluctuate with the inconsistencies of our efforts to engage in those activities which foster that relationship. But God's love cannot fluctuate, for we have a union with Christ that nothing can separate."
~ Bill Kynes, senior pastor of Cornerstone Evangelical Free Church

- Hello beautiful! Search out a quiet place to enjoy the nearness of God today. If your children are using you as a jungle gym, give them some dry cereal and take a deep breath; you are teaching them what is important, and they are soaking up your example. Read John 15:1-17, and write your favorite verse from that passage on a post-it note or index card to bring God's Word with you into every room today.

- I encourage you, if you have time, to look each Scripture up in your own Bible. Flipping through the actual pages helps me to log the message into my mind more permanently.

I Am NOT Enough

By: Stephanie Sandretto

The multitude of ways to celebrate Christmas usually leaves me paralyzed and unable to sort through which ones are "special enough" for recognizing Jesus' birth, until this year. This year was different. Before taking a project on, I stopped and asked God for His direction. I knew He would lead me because I was lost in the chaos without Him. When I researched, I found! I prepared, and then I enjoyed! I felt good. My three daughters were learning and loving the Advent journey exactly as I had hoped they would during this season, and it wasn't me who had brought it about. Peace was present in my home because I had purposed to abide by God's direction. Luke 2:14 sang in my head, "Glory to God in the highest, and on earth peace to men on whom his favor rests."

This incredible peace covered me until the last day before returning home from our first of two visits to Texas. My heart was burdened by a conflict that had arisen between the sides of my already separated family; each step throughout my morning had seemed like I was dragging cinder blocks across the floor. I stared at my husband and admitted dreading our return for Christmas Day only a week in the future.

Mama, are you there with me? Has this season wrapped you in great joy only to have the father of lies (John 8:44) weigh your heart down by burdens too heavy and cumbersome? Remember with me the soothing promise of Matthew 11:28, "Come to me, all you who are weary and burdened, and I will give you rest." At the beginning of this season, I knew I wasn't enough to make Christmas special, but when there was a conflict that I assumed I could handle on my own, my rest in God's direction ceased. My all-time favorite verse is Galatians 3:3 (NLT), "How foolish can you be? After starting your new lives in the Spirit, why are you now trying to become perfect by your own human effort?" Take a step back. Can you manifest the joy that Christ's birth brings by your own creativity? No. I find it disappointingly easy to pick up a burden with my own strength and step away from the Vine. I need to be constantly reminded of John 15:4, "Remain in me, as I also remain in you. No branch can bear fruit by itself; it must remain in the vine." Yet if I just as easily recognize my need to stay in communion with Jesus, my joy will be made complete, just as in John 15:11, "I have told you this so that my joy may be in you and that your joy may be complete."

Yes, the conflict remains waiting to be resolved when I venture back across Colorado, New Mexico, and deep into the heart of Texas. Fortunately, God isn't relying on my ability to create peace for my family. I encourage you, precious daughter of God, that you are not expected to be enough for what is ahead of you. Jeremiah 31:9 reminds us of God's heart toward His people, "I will lead them beside streams of water on a level path where they will not stumble." Let us not wander from our Vine who lavishly covers us in His peace and strength, moment by moment.

Questions to Ponder

• What are your thoughts throughout the day? Are you in constant conversation with God? Where do your thoughts go when conflict arises? What verses from God's Word can overcome the lies that you are being fed?

Faith-Filled Ideas

When I saw that my mind wasn't in communion with God, Psalm 19:14 is what I clung to. It's written on an index card that has been carried in my back pocket, stuck to my bathroom mirror, and recited a thousand times. Psalm 19:14 states, "May these words of my mouth and this meditation of my heart be pleasing in your sight, LORD, my Rock, and my Redeemer." Try writing a verse and bringing it with you. Speak the verse out loud; this habit will remind you and Satan that he has no place in your mind.

Here are more Scriptures that can encourage you to abide in God's strength, no matter what conflict you face:

• **Isaiah 54:10:** "'Though the mountains be shaken and the hills be removed, yet my unfailing love for you will not be shaken nor my covenant of peace be removed,' says the LORD, who has compassion on you."

• **Philippians 4:6-7:** "Do not be anxious about anything, but in every situation, by prayer and petition, with thanksgiving, present your requests to God. And the peace of God, which transcends all understanding, will guard your hearts and your minds in Christ Jesus."

journal

_____

_____

_____

_____

_____

journal

_____

_____

_____

_____

_____

_____

_____

_____

_____

_____

_____

_____

_____

_____

_____

_____

_____

_____

_____

_____

_____

_____

_____

_____

_____

Christmas

Christmas ~ Week Four ~ Day Eleven

> **"** There's a boy here who has five barley loaves and two fish—
> but what are they for so many? **"**
>
> ~ John 6:9 (HCSB)

"We are not called to be successful, we are called to be faithful."
~ Mother Teresa

- Dear one, Jesus can't wait to meet with you, in your warm, fuzzy socks, snuggled into your cozy blanket and under the glow of the Christmas lights.

- Please read John 6:1-11 and write verse 9 in your journal. Pray that the Holy Spirit would speak to your heart as you read God's Word.

Abiding in Jesus

By: Susan Proctor

This miracle in John chapter 6 isn't a typical Christmas Bible story. However, this familiar passage about the power of the Holy Spirit has encouraged me this Christmas season. In the midst of Christmas last year, my family was suffering with sickness, a husband preparing for deployment on New Year's Eve, and a chronically ill child with several medical appointments.

I was unable to do all the fun things that I had imagined and planned. I had nothing left at the end of the day; I was mentally and physically exhausted. I was silently suffering and feeling like a failure. In all honesty, I thought I was letting God down because we weren't doing all the "Christian" Christmas activities. That is when the Holy Spirit spoke to me through John chapter 6.

Jesus had compassion on the crowd, desiring to satisfy their hunger. Jesus didn't need the 5 loaves of bread and two fish to feed them. He was completely capable of creating food out of nothing. Yet, He took what they had, mixed with the optimistic faith of Andrew (the disciple who told Him about the five loaves and two fish), to miraculously feed over 5,000 people! Jesus wants to meet our needs too. When we abide in God and give Him all that we have, His power overcomes our weaknesses.

As Christmas approaches, let's practice abiding in God and give Him what we have. He will, in return, work miracles. Abiding in Jesus and in His love brings the peace and power God sent His son to impart.

Our Christmas was different this year: no Christmas cards were sent, we only had two desserts for Christmas dinner, Jesus' birthday cake was never decorated, tours of neighborhood Christmas lights didn't happen as often, and our tree was without presents until 11 p.m. Christmas Eve. However, we played games, read books, and listened to stories together, making unforgettable family memories. Instead of watching the fun from the kitchen, I joined my sweet children on the floor as they explored their new toys. I experienced their joyful expressions and hugged them longer. My husband and I even snuggled up together to watch *It's a Wonderful Life*. I chose to abide in Jesus and let Him take my five loaves of bread and two fish to make this Christmas magical.

Questions to Ponder

- Are you feeling overwhelmed?

- Has your Christmas season been more about checking something off or spending quality time with God and those you love?

- Do you need to make some adjustments and give yourself grace?

Faith-Filled Ideas

Dear sweet moms, have you taken your schedule, your craft list, and your Christmas shopping list before God? After writing out the activities, events, and shopping you and your family want to accomplish, listen to Him direct your path, one step at a time, about His desires for your family. Throughout each day, be open and flexible as God brings unexpected opportunities.

"Wait for the Lord; be strong and courageous. Wait for the Lord." Psalm 27:14 (HCBS)

journal

Hosting families during the holidays is one of my favorite pastimes! I love the lights and laughs and festive décor! I always want to have pretty snack foods out on display so they can be sampled and savored while visiting. This Holiday Cheese Ball is perfect for entertaining, and even more perfect to tote to someone else's party! I especially like how easy this recipe is to make!

HOLIDAY CHEESE BALL   By: Rae-Ellen Sanders

Ingredients:

2 packages of cream cheese, at room temperature

8 ounces of crumbled feta cheese

1-2 cloves of garlic

1 (10-ounce) box of frozen, chopped spinach,
  thawed and well-drained

1 jar of artichokes, drained and chopped

2 jars of roasted red peppers, drained
  and chopped

Equipment you will need:

Mixing bowl, medium glass bowl, spatula, garlic press, chopping device or food processor, paper towels, and clear plastic wrap.

Directions:

1. Combine cream cheese and feta cheese in mixing bowl. Press garlic and mix together.

2. Using paper towels, press off excess moisture from spinach.

3. Chop artichokes into small pieces with a processor, drain well, and add together with spinach and cream cheese. Mix well with spatula.

4. Repeat chopping of peppers, drain well, and pat dry. Set aside.

5. Line glass bowl with plastic wrap.

6. Start layering by adding half of the cheese-spinach mixture on top of plastic wrap (in the bottom of the bowl), pressing down into the plastic wrap, and shaping the ball.

7. Add red peppers on top of cheese-spinach mixture and press lightly so the peppers don't bleed into the cheese.

8. Spread remaining layer of the cheese-artichoke-spinach mixture onto the ball.

9. Fold over plastic wrap and refrigerate—one hour is sufficient, but longer will allow the flavors to blend better.

10. When ready to serve, turn glass bowl upside down on serving plate. The cheese mold should invert to a colorful, layered mound of yummy goodness!

11. Decorate with crackers of your choosing around your Holiday Cheese Mold, dig in, and *enjoy!*

New Year's

Happy New Year, Mamas!

With a New Year comes a fresh start!

Let me encourage you to take a few minutes to write down one or two things you'd like to accomplish this year.

I've found that *writing* ideas down will help make them happen.

After you've written your goals for the year, request prayer for those things. Ask your prayer partner to pray and consider sharing your goals on our Monday morning Facebook prayer request post in our Help Club for Moms Online Group. We will pray for you there! If you're not yet a member, be sure to ask to be added. It's a great group!

Lastly, ask someone to keep you accountable to stay committed to achieving your goal(s).

I've found that those three steps make all the difference in completing what I've started:

1. Write it down
2. Pray
3. Be accountable

Your goal may be to consistently spend time with your heavenly Father, having a regular date night with your husband, or starting something you've been putting off. This year, with God's help and someone "pushing you along," your dreams can be a reality!

May this be your *best year yet!!*

Blessings and love,
Kathryn Egly and the Help Club For Moms Team

> *And the LORD answered me: 'Write the vision;*
> *make it plain on tablets, so he may run who reads it.*
> *~ Habakkuk 2:2*

*"I am the vine; you are the branches. If you remain
in me and I in you, you will bear much fruit..."* ~ John 15:5

The Wise Woman Builds Her Spirit

- Pray and ask the Lord to help you to be the wise woman who builds her house (Proverbs 14:1). What do you want to build into your family this year? What do you want each room of your "house" to contain; kindness, encouragement, prayer, praise, service, self-discipline? We must be intentional about what we want to "build" into our "house" or our family this year! If you want to get creative, sketch out a simple house outline with rooms, detailing what you are planning to build into the lives and hearts of your home and family this year!

- Make time to exercise this week. It's important to take care of our bodies!

The Wise Woman Loves Her Husband

- Give your husband a free night this week. Encourage him to connect face to face with a friend.

- Plan a "Triple-Five-Night" with your husband this week. Share five of your favorite memories or accomplishments from the past year, five goals for the new year, and five things you are looking forward to in the coming year. Try this with your kids too!

The Wise Woman Loves Her Children

- Create a prayer list specific to each of your children to pray for the next year. Choose specific items and areas of growth to commit to the Lord in prayer. Put your list in your prayer binder for reference.

- Have a New Year's party with your family! Make your family's favorite foods, look at pictures or watch home movies of your past year, thank God for all the blessings of this past year and pray for the coming year!

The Wise Woman Cares For Her Home

- Take time to write thank you notes for the gifts you received for Christmas. Use the last 10 minutes of your quiet time to write one or two a day until you are finished.

- Ask your family what meals they love the most and make your own family cookbook of your favorites. Make sure to repeat them often in the New Year and add more as you discover them.

He who says he abides in Him ought himself also to walk just as He walked.

~ 1 John 2:6 (NKJV)

"Instead of making a New Year's resolution, consider committing to a biblical solution."

~ Mary Fairchild

New Year's

- Take a moment to push the "pause" button and pray with your prayer partner. Pray together to ask the Lord to help you and your family to stay healthy and strong as you finish time with family and friends, begin taking down your decorations and simply recover. Ask God to help you remember the good from your holiday season.

- Dear sister, as another year is drawing to a close, it is time to ponder resolutions. Resolutions involve laying aside what didn't work out so well and making a strategic plan to make the New Year prosper. As Christian writer Mary Fairchild says, "Instead of a resolution, commit to a biblical solution." Take a minute right now and ask the Lord to reveal to you any changes He wants you to make in your life. Jot down what you hear in your journal, and then grab your Bible for a very interactive Bible Study using the letters of the alphabet! This study has us delving into Scriptures that will guide us in the way we should live!

A Biblical Solution to Resolutions

By: Rae-Ellen Sanders

Wow, hasn't this "Wise Woman Abides" study just blessed your socks off? I have truly learned to love the word "abide." There is no better place to be than in the arms of Jesus and in His presence! I pray that you have been encouraged in your mothering and that you feel equipped with the knowledge that God will supply your needs as you lean on His Holy Spirit.

Just like 1 John 2:6 states above, if we abide in Christ, we will want to walk like Christ. Personally, I plan to be proactive in the new year, especially with memorizing Scripture and having the Word of God stored up in my heart. I hope this alphabet "solution" will inspire you to walk out your faith, too.

A – *Abide in Jesus*
John 15:4, 1 John 3:24

B – *Bread of life—Dine on it Daily*
John 6:51, John 6:35

C – *Confession*
1 John 1:9, James 5:16

D – *Do Unto Others*
Matthew 7:12

E – *Evangelize*
2 Timothy 4:1-2, Mark 16:15

F – *Forgive*
Matthew 6:15, Ephesians 1:7

G – *Glorify*
1 Corinthians 6:20, Psalm 86:12

H – *Hope*
Hebrews 6:19, Romans 5:5

I – *Instruction*
Proverbs 23:12, Proverbs 4:13

J – *Justice*
Isaiah 1:17, Zechariah 7:9

K – *Kindness*
Colossians 3:12-13

L – *Love One Another*
John 13:34-35, Romans 12:10

M – *Meditate on God's Word*
Joshua 1:8, Psalm 119:27

N – *New Life*
2 Corinthians 5:17

O – *Obey the Voice of the Lord*
Deuteronomy 13:4, Deuteronomy 28:1

P – *Prayer*
Philippians 4:6, 1 Peter 3:12

Q – *Quiet spirit*
1 Peter 3:3-4, Isaiah 32:17

R – *Receive the Holy Spirit*
Colossians 2:6-7, 1 Corinthians 2:12

S – *Serve with Righteousness, Peace, and Joy*
Romans 14:17-18, Psalm 100:2

T – *Trust*
Proverbs 3:5-6

U – *Unashamed*
Romans 1:16, 2 Timothy 2:15

V – *Victorious in Faith*
1 John 5:4b, 1 Corinthians 15:57

W – *Worship*
Psalm 95:6, 1 Chronicles 16:29

X – *Ten Commandments*
Deuteronomy 10:12, Exodus 20:1-17

Y – *Yield*
James 3:17

Z – *Zealous*
Proverbs 23:17, Proverbs 8:13

Questions to Ponder

• Have you been reading the Word of God daily? If you haven't been dining on the **B**-Bread of Life/ Word of God, now is the time to make this your first change in the new year. The Bible says in Matthew 4:4, "But He answered and said, "It is written, 'Man shall not live by bread alone, but by every word that proceeds from the mouth of God.'" Make a decision to adopt a daily Bible reading plan starting on January 1st. You can find many of them on Bible apps or in devotional books.

• How are you doing in the arena of **K**-Kindness and **S**-Service? Have you been **D**-Doing Unto Others or **L**-Loving Others in the power of the Holy Spirit this past year? These verses encourage us to turn from a mediocre Christian walk to a **G**-Glorious one! If you aren't familiar with **C**-Confessing your sins, try it this year. You will experience inner healing and God's **F**-Forgiveness. **P**-Prayer and **R**-Receiving the Holy Spirit will undoubtedly give you **N**-New life! **T**-Trusting your steps to the Lord and leaning not on your own understanding will give you the bonus of a **Q**-Quiet and **Y**-Yielding spirit.

• Do you hear the **V**-Voice of God? **A**-Abiding and spending time with the Father will increase your ability to discern His still, small voice. **M**-Meditating on God's faithfulness and Scripture will give you **H**-Hope, fill you with knowledge, and set you up for success. **O**-Obeying His Voice and observing the **X**-Ten Commandments will lead you toward **J**-Justice and a **V**-Victorious life!

Faith-Filled Ideas

Make a plan to memorize Scripture to store it up to refresh your soul. When an opportunity arises to share the good news, you'll be able to **E**-Evangelize openly without hesitation or fear. Take each acrostic listed above and commit to memorizing one Bible verse a week. 45 Scriptures will put you all the way into November!

Print and laminate them, add to a keychain or carabiner for easy reference or write them out in a journal for daily reflection. Utilize a chalkboard/dry erase board at home so your family can join you with Bible memorization! Ask your kids to quiz you, and impart the importance of seeking **I**-Instruction. **W**-Worship the Lord as you succeed. I pray there are a lot of praise parties in your home this year. Continue to be **U**-Unashamed and **Z**-Zealous for God's Word in the new year!

Journal

_____

_____

_____

_____

_____

_____

_____

_____

_____

_____

_____

_____

_____

_____

_____

_____

_____

_____

_____

_____

_____

> Unless the LORD builds the house, those who build it labor in vain. Unless the LORD watches over the city, the watchman stays awake in vain.

~ Psalm 127:1 (ESV)

"What you get by achieving your goals is not as important as what you become by achieving your goals."
~ Zig Ziglar

- Dear friend, come soak in the presence of your heavenly Father today. Read Psalm 127:1. If you have time, read the entire chapter.

What's the Word?

By: Rebekah Measmer

As one year closes and another year opens, like books in a series, we eagerly anticipate all that the New Year has in store. Many make new resolutions or goals, since without objectives, we wander aimlessly, arrows without a target. In need of direction, I set yearly expectations for myself with a slightly different approach. Believing that without a solid foundation nothing will stand, I pray and ask God what *His* yearly word or theme is for me. This word or theme serves as a guide for the coming year. For example, for three years in a row "rest" was the word God gave to me. Why so many repeated years? I believe it took three years for me to finally begin practicing what He knew I needed to do! This past year, the word was "focus." *Focus* on Him. *Focus* on His Word. *Focus* on my family. *Focus* on my marriage. *Focus* on each day...on each moment. *Focus* this year and anticipate all that He has in store.

"That's great," you may think, "but how am I to discover my word for the year?" God speaks to each person, using different methods at times, but He *does* speak. The most obvious way to find out is simply to pray and ask God what He wants your goal to be for this year. I find that when I quiet myself, listen, and patiently wait, He brings a word to my mind; it could be a Scripture verse, a sentence, perhaps lyrics from a hymn, or a picture. Another way to discover your aim for the year is by opening your Bible, which is living and active (Hebrews 4:12), and ask Him to highlight a Scripture for you. Anytime we read our Bibles, the Creator of All is speaking to us because the Bible is not some collection of ancient writings by philosophical men, but God-breathed (2 Timothy 3:16) and timeless. God speaks to each person, using various ways, but He *does* speak.

When you have received your word, Scripture, or theme, write it down where you will see it each day. Fervently pray for God to reveal the areas in your life where He is specifically speaking this word to you. This may happen gradually over the year, so have patience as He unveils your eyes and heart to areas of your life where He wishes to have your attention. Finally, listen daily for Him to speak as you both proclaim and humbly ask, "Lord, my day is yours. Fill me with your Holy Spirit. What are You doing today, and how can I cooperate?" His Word will be your daily foundation to build upon this year, your filter with which to look at each chapter in this wonderful new "book."

Questions to Ponder

• Is my aim for this year to bring Him glory or to bring glory to myself?

• Am I laying a good foundation for the new year by prayerfully seeking God's goals for me, or am I choosing my own goals based on trends or self-serving desires?

• Have I thanked God for all that He has done for me and my family during the past twelve months?

Faith-Filled Ideas

Buy an inexpensive miniature chalkboard and write your word or Scripture for the year on it in a pretty font. Hang or display your new art in an area of your home that you frequent, so you will see it often throughout each day. Each time you see it, breathe a quick prayer to your Father, asking Him to guide you moment by moment.

Ask God for a word or Scripture for your spouse and each of your children or a theme for you as a family. If your children are in upper elementary school or older, encourage them to pray and seek God for their own word or Scripture for the new year. There is no such thing as a "junior Holy Spirit." God speaks to everyone who asks Him, both young and old alike.

Carve out extra time one evening this week to remember and celebrate all that God has done for your family in the past year. Encourage each family member to share their favorite part of that year, the most difficult part of that year, and their goal(s) for the next year. Questions can vary depending upon age and understanding. Write each answer down as you go, or record the answers on a voice memo app as a keepsake, as well as a reminder. Consider making this "New Year's Remember and Celebrate" ceremony a new family tradition. Keep it simple or be ultra-creative—you do you!

journal

Journal

And He said, 'Come.' And Peter, having descended from the boat,
walked upon the water and came to Jesus.

~ Matthew 14:29 (Berean Literal Bible)

"Though the road be rough and stormy,
Trackless as the foaming sea,
Thou hast trod this way before me,
And I gladly follow Thee.
I will follow Thee, my Savior,
Thou didst shed Thy blood for me;
And though all men should forsake Thee,
By Thy grace I'll follow Thee.."

~ James Elginburg, *I Will Follow Thee* (1871)

- You've done it. You have moved toward your Savior and He sees you. Grab your Bible and enjoy Matthew 14:25-33. Record verse 29 in your journal or on your index cards. Meditate on taking that first step to obey Jesus. Let us remember that He wants us to walk with Him; His hand is extended toward you, mama.

Walking on Water

By: Stephanie Sandretto

I'm a sucker for new things. Even grocery shopping thrills me. Be it a bag of apples or rolls of toilet paper, the newness awakens my appreciation for life. The New Year is no exception. When I sit down with a planner to look at the year ahead, I see a book overflowing with possibilities. At times, I'm filled with anticipation paralysis. I imagine Peter took that first step into the water with a mixture of wonder and fear, yet he still took it. He obeyed the call of his friend, his Master, and He walked on water!

Peter moved toward the new and unknown because he saw Jesus in front of him. We read in the Bible how God calls us to new things (Isaiah 43:19) and loves bringing us new mercies every day (Lamentations 3:22-23)! When we step into something new, we are not alone. Today you get to choose to step out of the boat and move toward Jesus or to stay where you are. Your choice to obey should be based not on what happened yesterday, but by the fresh start Christ offers you right now.

Listen to Oswald Chambers' challenge in *My Utmost for His Highest*: "Loyalty to Jesus means I have to step out where I do not see anything (Matthew 14:29); loyalty to my notions means that I clear the ground first by my intelligence. Faith is not intellectual understanding, faith is deliberate commitment to a Person where I see no way."

Peter, as an intelligent man, could have thought of many reasons why he wanted to stay in the boat. Friends, stop planning your obedience. You will second guess each action until you have completely forgotten about Christ's extended hand of help and direction. John 2:5 (BLB) reminds me of the simplicity of our obedience when Mary directs, "Whatever He may say to you, do it." Do it. This first step must be "deliberate commitment...where [you] see no way" (Oswald Chambers, *My Utmost for His Highest*).

There is no doubt that Peter only began to sink once the waves became his focus, not Jesus. Unlike Peter who started to sink when he took his eyes off Jesus, may we keep our eyes on Jesus and make obedience our goal! Be encouraged by John 8:12, "... I am the light of the world. Whoever follows me will never walk in darkness, but will have the light of life." Friends, Jesus wants to walk with you. He wants you to invite Him into your day and to let the Holy Spirit change the way you respond to Him in faith.

After reading James 1:19-20, where Scripture exhorts us to be quick to listen and slow to anger, I realized that I had to learn how to step out in a deliberate commitment of faith in my own life. Letting go of my anger wasn't comfortable and my temper raged. My anger was creating a crisis in our home. I wasn't acting like the woman of God that I longed to be. Becoming slow to anger was foreign and uncomfortable; anger made me feel as though I was strong. But God was calling me to surrender to Him. By reading God's Word, I learned that I could feel strong and didn't need to hold on to aggression. Leaving my past behind and moving forward with God's Word, equipped me and strengthened me.

2 Corinthians 10:4-5 says, "The weapons we fight with are not the weapons of the world. On the contrary, they have divine power to demolish strongholds. We demolish arguments and every pretension that sets itself up against the knowledge of God, and we take captive every thought to make it obedient to Christ."

Questions to Ponder

- The New Year always represents a fresh start. In what area do you feel God is asking you to step out in faith like Peter? What is your "something new?" Where have you held back in obedience to Christ this last year, and how will you move toward obedience now? Who do you need to apologize to or hold yourself accountable to as you change?

Faith-Filled Ideas

Christ wants to assure us as His children that He is for us and not against us. Memorizing Scripture helped me to focus on where God was leading me. Here are verses to give you strength in your fight for new growth:

- Isaiah 41:13, "For I am the LORD your God who takes hold of your right hand and says to you, 'Do not fear; I will help you.'"
- James 1:2-4, "Consider it pure joy, my brothers and sisters, whenever you face trials of many kinds, because you know that the testing of your faith produces perseverance. Let perseverance finish its work so that you may be mature and complete, not lacking anything."
- Isaiah 40:31, "But those who hope in the LORD will renew their strength. They will soar on wings like eagles; they will run and not grow weary, they will walk and not be faint."

journal

_____

_____

_____

_____

journal

Journal

New Year's

Help Club For Moms is a group of real moms who seek to grow closer to God, closer to our families, and closer to each other. We believe prayer changes everything and God is big enough to help us raise the children with whom God has blessed us.

We focus on digging into God's Word, praying together, and encouraging one another! Through weekly "Mom Tips" and daily "Faith Filled Ideas," the Help Club for Moms helps women take what they are learning about the Lord and apply it to their daily journey as wives and mothers. Our goal is to spread the love of Jesus, inspire women to be the wives and mothers God created us to be and to impact eternity—One mama at a time!

Would you like to be a part of the movement?

Here's how you can get involved in the Help Club for Moms:

- *The Wise Woman Builds, The Wise Woman Cares, The Wise Woman Enjoys, The Wise Woman Knows, The Wise Woman Loves, The Wise Woman Stays,* and *The Joy Challenge for Moms* by Help Club For Moms are available on Amazon.

- Pray for the ministry and the moms in our Help Club Community worldwide—for them to know the love of Jesus and create a Christ-Like atmosphere in their homes.

- Start a Help Club for Moms group at your local church or home. We can help you!

- We are always on the lookout for Titus 2 women who can help mentor our moms through social media and prayer.

- If you are an author, blogger, graphics artist, or social media guru, we need you and your talents at the Help Club!

- We are a 501(c)(3) and all volunteer ministry! Please go to www.HelpClubForMoms.com to help us get God's Word into the hands of moms worldwide!

Questions? Email us at info@helpclubformoms.com.
You can find out more about Help Club for Moms at www.HelpClubForMoms.com and
on Facebook and Instagram @HelpClubForMoms.

Church Resource Section

Moms encouraging moms to know the love of Christ

Dear Mom,

We are so very honored that you are journeying through this Bible study with us. What a gift you are to our ministry!

We wanted to make sure you knew that, built right into this book, is everything you need to start a "Help Club for Moms" group of your own! You can do it through your church or even as a small group in your home. Lives are changed when we read God's Word together and focus on becoming intentional moms and wives in community together! Doing a Help Club for Moms Bible Study is a chance for you and your friends to dive deeper into learning about God's design for motherhood. Plus, everything is more fun with friends!

It is so easy to lead a Help Club for Moms group. Each mom commits to following along in the Bible study. Then you meet at your home or church just twice per month to go over what you are learning and pray for one another. We even have a special group on Facebook dedicated to our Help Club for Moms Bible Study Leaders where we mentor you and give you ideas for your own group. It is wonderful!

Doing life together as moms in a Christ-centered community draws us closer to Jesus and to each other while building friendship and connections that are sure to last a lifetime. What a great way to walk as moms, together arm-in-arm and with our eyes on Jesus, all the way until we get to heaven.

If you are interested in starting a Help Club for Moms group, either in your church or home, please email us at info@helpclubformoms.com. We would love to walk alongside you, give you helpful resources, and PRAY for you.

Blessings to you, mama!

Sincerely,

The Help Club for Moms Team

FAQ:
About Help Club For Moms

WHAT IS THE HELP CLUB FOR MOMS?

• Help Club for Moms is a community of moms encouraging moms to know the love of Christ. We value authentic, transparent relationships. Together, we study God's Word, pray, fellowship twice a month, and share practical "Mom Tips." All this to become the women, wives, and mothers God created us to be, and with the help of the Holy Spirit, bring up our children to do the same!

WHY CHOOSE HELP CLUB?

• Help Club For Moms offers a Christ-centered program focused on strengthening the church by strengthening moms, through teaching God's design for families and biblically based parenting.

• There is no fee for the program; the only cost is for the books which may be purchased on Amazon.

• The program is for moms of all ages. We love learning from each other in every stage of life!

• There are three simple, but deep, biblical studies per week, which teach and encourage moms, yet are still easy to accomplish. A must for today's busy mom!

• Help Club For Moms "Mom Tips" set us apart from other mom groups because every week, we offer eight practical, new ideas to strengthen and train women in their role as a wife, mother, and woman of God.

• Each mom in Help Club For Moms is partnered with another mom for prayer. Every week, these two moms pray for 10-15 minutes with one another over the phone, deepening their connection with God and each other. Prayer changes everything!

• Help Club For Moms brings godly community, support, fellowship, and friendship to families through the relationships formed between moms.

• HCFMs has three years of Christ-Centered curriculum.

• HCFM has a strong presence on social media, which helps moms go deeper in the studies with other moms around the world.

WHAT ARE THE CORE VALUES OF HELP CLUB FOR MOMS?

• HCFM values authentic and transparent community between moms, deep growth in relationship with God, intentional Bible study, faithful prayer relationships between moms, and practical day-to-day ideas and tips for moms.

WHAT IS REQUIRED OF THE CHURCH?

• HCFMs partner churches should plan to help in two ways:

    1. Offer a meeting space for two hours/twice monthly

    2. Help with childcare for two hours/twice monthly

Hosting a HCFM's Meeting

WHAT DOES A TYPICAL HELP CLUB FOR MOMS MEETING LOOK LIKE?

• Hosting a Help Club meeting is easy and fun and is a great way to build community with the moms in your church or neighborhood. Below is a sample morning meeting schedule. (You could also host a "Help Club Mom's Night Out Potluck Dinner" instead of a daytime meeting for working moms or moms who want some time away while dad has the children.)

SCHEDULE

9:30-9:40   Welcome, pray, and on time drawing with an inexpensive prize

9:40-10:15   **Moms meet in groups to discuss current HCFM Bible study**
- Large groups: Moms sit around tables in small groups of 3-6 moms with a leader and possible co-leader to discuss content from the last two week's topic.
- Small groups or home study group: Moms sit in a circle as one big group to discuss content from the last two week's topic.

10:15-10:30   **Simple worship and announcements** (HCFM Spotify and Amazon Prime playlist and lyrics provided if desired)

10:30-10:35   **Book Review** (HCFM suggested book review provided if desired)

10:35-10:50   **Mom Tips in Action** (Invite one of your leaders/ helpers to spotlight a Mom Tip from this week's study and how she used it) Then, invite other moms from the group to share how they used a moms tip from the list or how they are planning to use one in the future. This is an important time for our moms to learn from each other.

10:50-11:15   **Devotion time**
There are two ways to facilitate a HCFM's devotion portion of the group: one led by a seasoned mom or one led by a young, peer aged mom.
- Both groups lead a discussion about the topic from the last two weeks of study by discussing Scripture and asking questions of the group about the topic. (Scripture applicable to the topic and "Questions to Ponder" are found in each study.) The leader shares her personal experiences as a fellow mom journeying on the road of motherhood. The leader may also choose to watch a portion of a Help Club for Moms "Mentoring Monday" video about the topic with the moms in her group.

11:15-11:25   **Moms pray with prayer partners**

11:25   **Pray and dismiss moms to pick up children**

All HCFM leaders have access to a private Facebook group (Help Club for Moms National Group Leaders) where they can access training videos, ask questions, and share ideas to help them host a successful group. **Questions? Email us at info@helpclubformoms.com.**

Book Recommendations

BOOKS FOR MOMS (NON-FICTION):

Parenting the Wholehearted Child
  by Jeannie Cunnion

You and Me by Francis and Lisa Chan (marriage)

Daring Greatly by Brene Brown

The Ragamuffin Gospel by Brennan Manning

Love and Respect by Dr. Emmerson Eggerichs

Love and Respect in the family
  by Dr. Emmerson Eggerichs

Mother and Son by Dr. Emmerson Eggerichs

The Circle Maker by Mark Batterson

The Power of a Praying Wife
  by Stormie O' Martian

The Power of a Praying Parent
  by Stormie O' Martian

The Read-Aloud Family by Sarah Mackenzie

BOOKS FOR MOMS (FICTION):

Mark of the Lion trilogy by Francine Rivers

Redeeming Love by Francine Rivers

Sarah's Key by Tatiana de Rosnay

The Help by Kathryn Stockett

BOOKS FOR KIDS:

Discipleship books:

The Picture Bible published by David C. Cook

The Jesus Storybook Bible by Sally Lloyd-Jones

The Action Bible by Sergio Cariello

Missionary Stories with the Millers
  by Mildred A. Martin

Upper Elementary/Early Middle School (grades 4-7):

The Wingfeather Saga by Andrew Peterson

The Green Ember series by E.D. Smith

The Penderwicks series by Jeanne Birdsall

Lower Elementary (grades 2-3):

The Imagination Station by Marianne Hering

Greetings from Somewhere by Harper Paris

Dear Molly, Dear Olive by Megan Atwood

Early Readers (grades K-1):

Owl Diaries by Rebecca Elliot

I Can Read! Princess Parables by Jeanna Young

Jotham's Journey series

Little House on the Prairie by Laura Ingalls Wilder

The BFG by Roald Dahl

The Lion, The Witch, and the Wardrobe
  by C.S. Lewis

Anne of Green Gables by Lucy Maud Montgomery

HOMESCHOOLING:

Teaching From Rest by Sarah Mackenzie

Educating the WholeHearted Child
  by Clay Clarkson with Sally Clarkson

Seasons of a Mother's Heart by Sally Clarkson

Podcasts

PODCASTS FOR MOMS:

God Centered Mom

Coffee & Crumbs

Java with Juli

Cultivating the Lovely

The Inspired to Action Podcast

Parenting Great Kids with Dr. Meg Meeker

Focus on the Family

The Messenger Podcast

Conversations with John and Lisa Bevere

I am Adamant Podcast by Lisa Bevere

PODCASTS FOR KIDS:

Stories Podcast

Storynory

Brains On! Science Podcast for Kids

Adventures in Odyssey

Read Aloud Revival

ONLINE SERMONS:

ChurchoftheHighlands.org

Theaterchurch.org

Worship Music

PANDORA HELP CLUB FOR MOMS STATION:

https://pdora.co/2KynyvV

SPOTIFY HELP CLUB FOR MOMS STATION:

https://spoti.fi/2lVBMbw

Daily Plan

Date:_____

M T W T F S S

Weekly Memory Verse:

"

"

3 Things I am Grateful for Today:

1.

2.

3.

Notes:

6 Most Important List:

1.

2.

3.

4.

5.

6.

Meal Planning:

Breakfast:

Lunch:

Dinner:

Cleaning:

O 15-min. area _____

O 5'o clock pick-up

Weekly Plan

	Sunday	Monday	Tuesday	Wednesday	Thursday	Friday	Saturday
6:00							
7:00							
8:00							
9:00							
10:00							
11:00							
12:00							
1:00							
2:00							
3:00							
4:00							
5:00							
6:00							
7:00							
8:00							
9:00							
10:00							

Daily Plan

Date:_____

M T W T F S S

Weekly Memory Verse:

"

"

3 Things I am Grateful for Today:

1.

2.

3.

Notes:

6 Most Important List:

1.

2.

3.

4.

5.

6.

Meal Planning:

Breakfast:

Lunch:

Dinner:

Cleaning:

O 15-min. area _____

O 5'o clock pick-up

Weekly Plan

	Sunday	Monday	Tuesday	Wednesday	Thursday	Friday	Saturday
6:00							
7:00							
8:00							
9:00							
10:00							
11:00							
12:00							
1:00							
2:00							
3:00							
4:00							
5:00							
6:00							
7:00							
8:00							
9:00							
10:00							

Made in the USA
Coppell, TX
24 September 2020